101 Ways
FENG
SHUI
Can Change Your Life

Nancilee Wydra, FSII

Contemporary Books

*Chicago   New York   San Francisco   Lisbon   London   Madrid   Mexico City
Milan   New Delhi   San Juan   Seoul   Singapore   Sydney   Toronto*

Library of Congress Cataloging-in-Publication Data

Wydra, Nancilee.
    101 ways feng shui can change your life / Nancilee Wydra.
        p.   cm.
    Includes bibliographical references and index.
    ISBN 0-07-138138-4
    1. Feng shui.   I. Title: One hundred one ways feng shui can change
your life.   II. Title: One hundred and one ways feng shui can change your
life.   III. Title.

BF1779.F4 W9   2002
133.3'337—dc21   2002019311

Contemporary Books

*A Division of The **McGraw-Hill** Companies*

2 3 4 5 6 7 8 9 0 FGR/FGR 1 0 9 8 7 6 5

ISBN 0-07-138138-4

This book was set in Adobe Garamond by Rattray Design
Printed and bound by Quebecor Fairfield

Cover design by Monica Baziuk
Cover photographs copyright © Gettyimages
Interior illustrations by Ginny Piech Street

McGraw-Hill books are available at special quantity discounts to use as premiums
and sales promotions, or for use in corporate training programs. For more
information, please write to the Director of Special Sales, Professional Publishing,
McGraw-Hill, Two Penn Plaza, New York, NY 10121-2298. Or contact your local
bookstore.

This book is printed on acid-free paper.

CONTENTS

Other books by Nancilee Wydra

Feng Shui: The Book of Cures
Feng Shui in the Garden
Feng Shui and How to Look Before You Love
Feng Shui Goes to the Office
Feng Shui for Children's Spaces
Feng Shui Principles for Building and Remodeling

PREFACE

Do you want to lose weight or alleviate feelings of depression? Are you looking to improve your love life or your relationship with your children? Do you wish you could extend your energy level or find a way to unwind? Feng shui may hold the answer. You can create an environment at home that will aid you in achieving many life goals.

Intuitively we all know it is impossible not to respond to our physical environment. No doubt you can remember visiting a place that was enchanting or experiencing an instant sense of unease upon crossing a particular threshold. Place affects how we feel and how we react. But we don't always understand how or why certain environments evoke certain feelings. Historically, Western culture has had no vocabulary or framework through which to interpret the messages that places deliver.

Feng shui, an ancient Chinese discipline, fills that gap. Still, many Westerners have difficulty transplanting classic feng shui into modern American and European culture. That's why I've devoted the last twenty-five years to the translation of feng shui principles for Western customs, philosophy, and culture. In my previous seven books on feng shui, I have shown how the findings of well-known social and physical scientists support feng shui's core messages. I have also illustrated how the principles of classic feng shui can be used to make your home a sanctuary, to make your garden help you thrive, to create an office that enhances your career, to shape nurturing, stimulating spaces for children to grow in, and more.

This book is a natural next step: ways to use feng shui to cure the modern ills that interfere with our lives and hamper our ability to reach our goals. Whether you need to reduce stress, increase self-confidence, or shrug off the blues, this book will lead you to the "cures" that can help. If you know the areas in life you wish to improve, you can flip to the chapters that offer suggestions for those areas. These suggestions are called *cures* because each remedies a life problem by adjusting your physical environment—a problem that might be preventing you from achieving a life goal. This book will reveal feng shui solutions for specific problems that you might be experiencing and help you alter behavior that is self-defeating. Take a look at your current circumstances and decide what aspects of yourself need to be enhanced, like self-esteem, and what needs to be adjusted, like weight, and then read the applicable section with the remedies that will stimulate change.

Consider feng shui a bag of tools to use for challenges you face. Feng shui is not magic; it is based on pragmatic evidence gathered from myriad social and physical sciences. For example, scientists have proved that when the color blue surrounds a person, his or her breathing and pulse rates slow down. Blue therefore works to calm. In situations that require you to take your time—be it to control your temper or refrain from taking that second helping of apple pie—blue in the environment can be an asset.

Feng shui is the language that describes why this is so. It is the key to decoding the messages we receive consciously and subconsciously from color, shape, patterns, scents, sounds, and textures. It is the tool we can use to manipulate the physical world around us to best suit our needs and desires. For example, from feng shui we know that chunky, earth-colored furniture shapes make people feel secure and hence can promote the ability to relax. If you are engaged in highly stressful work—as so many people are today—having a gathering space with a square, walnut-colored, wood, low-to-the-ground cocktail table could help you reduce stress by making you feel more secure.

Feng shui's underlying premise is that a home (or any other environment) can enhance or harm your chances for happiness. When it originated thousands of years ago, it grew out of the knowledge among early agrarian civilizations that information accumulated about the natural environment increased the chances of harvesting abundant crops. By understanding that spring floods cover the earth with enriched topsoil and that hurricanes, tornadoes, and earthquakes strike certain locations more frequently than others, the ancients laid the groundwork for a system of choosing the most felicitous environment. Over time, as knowledge of how place affects the human condition broadened, people learned not only how to choose the best environment for themselves but also how to create it. Today our home environments are complex and packed with contents. Feng shui is a key to sorting through it all to shape surroundings that will enhance happiness and future goals.

As an antidote to today's complex world and our multidimensional lives, I've attempted to make this book straightforward and uncomplicated. Each chapter addresses one of the modern ills that can be at the root of so much frustration and dissatisfaction, whether it is an emotional state such as depression or low self-esteem, a physical problem such as body weight, or a traumatic life event such as death or divorce. Each chapter breaks down the specific problem into manageable narrower solutions to install. To keep you focused on the potential for positive change, the cures are described via questions posed about how to implement solutions. If you're trying to alleviate depression, for example, Chapter 2 will answer questions about what colors cheer people, what patterns generate optimism, what patterns help people slough off unproductive old ways of thinking, and what you can add to your home to invigorate your mental attitude. You can choose the cures that you think you need most or implement them all one by one. Either way, you'll find the cures themselves are simple and easy on the pocket—not another way to complicate your life.

For centuries feng shui has been offering people ways to toss aside the factors in their lives that hinder their ability to thrive. Now it's your turn.

1

The Five Tools of Feng Shui

Every discipline is based on scientific principles. Feng shui is no exception. Just as physicians rely on test results to reassure them that their diagnosis is correct, the cures in this book are based on principles and data that have long been accepted as valid and rational. In feng shui, there are five different ways to break down and look at our world that help us decode the messages delivered by the places we live in. I think of them as tools, because they are used to determine which cures may be called for, just as a doctor uses various tests as diagnostic tools. But they are also the underpinnings of all of feng shui.

Since trust and belief are essential ingredients in change and healing, it makes sense for you to grasp these underpinnings of feng shui before you try to use feng shui to change your life. When you understand why something is true, you strengthen your intentions to use it.

Tao: Connections

The Tao (pronounced "Dow") means "the way things work." In the same way that the seasons follow each other year after year, there is a "way" that is normal and predictable for most of the world's natural processes. The sun rises and sets once every twenty-four hours, water flows downhill, and a fertilized egg follows a particular developmental path. It simply makes sense to go with that natural flow rather than fight it. Being in the Tao simply suggests understanding the natural order and going with its flow.

I use the word *connections* when evaluating the Tao of each situation. Being connected to the messages of color, shape, scent, touch, and positioning of the contents in our homes and using them to support what we want to feel is a way of being in the Tao and a way of using what surrounds us to further our goals. For example, if triangular shapes and the color red stimulate us and spark our intellect, as an understanding of chi tells us (see the discussion of chi a little later in this chapter), then seeing a triangle or the color red is likely to motivate us to do something, to take action rather than relax. A diamond-patterned red-toned wallpaper in the bedroom could be a barrier to relaxation and sleep.

Yin/Yang

Yin and yang represent the opposite extremes of any one process or concept. Examples of yin and yang are present throughout our lives. Things are cool or warm, alive or dead, active or passive, small or large in our frame of reference. We are either asleep or awake. Yin is like being asleep, when we are turned inward and typically do not interact with others. Yang is more like being awake, when we are typically interacting.

All colors, scents, sounds, and textures prod us to lean toward either yin or yang. When quiet or introspection is needed to assist with focus, when we have to gather ideas, be still, alone, or relaxed, a yin atmosphere is useful. When we want to communicate and need vigor to act, yang surroundings support us.

Most spaces will be a mixture of yin and yang. The question is what proportions of yin and yang make the right mix for a particular emotional experience. More yin would serve the rest and sleep needed in a bedroom, for example, while yang would benefit a gathering room, where lively conversation is usually desirable. The remedies in this book take this balancing act into consideration, using the following qualities to achieve the right mix for various needs.

Yin	*Yang*
Muted or light tones	Bright and fully saturated colors
Quiet, consistent sounds	Loud, varied sounds
Earthy or intense scents	Sharp or lightly fragrant scents
Smooth and soft textures	Rough and highly tactile textures
Low light levels	Bright lights
Quiet flooring that muffles footsteps	Flooring that resonates with footsteps
Absence of choices	Abundance of choices
Cramped or cluttered space	Enough room to move freely

CHI: HOW WE EXPERIENCE OUR WORLD

Probably the most used and least understood feng shui term is *chi*. Chi is often thought of as an amorphous entity living outside human experience, as if it had a life force of its own. It does not. For feng shui purposes *chi* is a word that describes our physical and emotional reactions to the physical world. We experience the world around us, both consciously and subconsciously, by seeing, hearing, smelling, touching, and moving through it. Therefore, the best way to understand chi is through the biology of the five senses.

Sight

Sight is our most utilized sense. Seventy percent of what we perceive is absorbed through vision. The human eye instantaneously seeks light, movement, diagonal lines, and the farthest distance when we enter an enclosed space. For that reason, much feng shui literature describes many conditions related to refracted light (crystals), windows, stairs (diagonal lines), and what is on the wall across from the entrance. What we see plays a substantial role in how we feel.

The colors and patterns that we see greatly influence how we feel about an environment, for they transmit emotional messages to us. In a general way, here's what they communicate:

Color/Shape	Message
Red/chevron, triangle	Excitement; sparks intellect
Yellow, tan, brown/square	Stability, safety
White, gold, silver/round	Mental churning, focus
Blue, black/wavy	Relaxation; unearths emotions, mystery, seduction
Green/rectangle	Change, learning

Other colors that are not related to specific shapes:

Color	Message
Orange	Fusion, cooperation
Purple	The unknown and its possibilities

When two colors are mixed, they dilute but still emit the messages of both colors. Also be aware that the deep colors or fully saturated colors affect us more physically, the midrange colors affect us more emotionally, and light colors affect us more intellectually or spiritually. Thus, when mental clarity is needed to absorb information, light yellow is better than medium or dark yellow.

Hearing

Our first sensory experience is sound. A fetus can hear before it can see or smell and before it acquires the brain function to move independently. In his book *The Mozart Effect*, Don Campbell writes,

"Sounds form patterns and create energy fields of resonance and movement in the surrounding space. We absorb these energies, and they subtly alter our breath, pulse, blood pressure, muscle tension, skin temperature and other internal rhythms." According to Campbell, music can boost immune functions, regulate stress-related hormones, change our perception of space and time, strengthen memory and learning, increase productivity, enhance romance and sexuality, stimulate digestion, foster endurance, augment unconscious receptivity to symbolism, and generate a sense of safety and well-being. Thus sound in all its forms is integral to our experience, and tapping its benefits makes good sense.

Smell

Scents communicate to us through a more primitive part of the brain than sight does. Our olfactory sense is the oldest we have, and smells are filtered through the part of the brain that responds and operates without conscious thought rather than the part that thinks and analyzes. Thus, with the exception of cultural and individual experiential differences, scents affect all humans similarly. Just as we can predict a medicine's effect on most people, the impression of a scent is foreseeable.

Touch

Infants who are not cuddled do not thrive. Babies abandoned by their birth mothers and placed in the care of an overworked hospital staff in a crowded facility might not get the necessary tactile stimulation within the first few days of life and will not develop as quickly and harmoniously as they would have with loving physical attention. Human physical contact is extremely important to well-being.

So are other tactile sensations. Textures communicate in the same ways as color, patterns, and scents. Yet in most cultures our skin, the largest sensory receptor, is covered up by clothing. This makes the tactile exposure we do experience even more important.

The Meaning of Scents

SCENT	EFFECTS
rose	strengthens spirit and love
lavender	calms; eases self-expression
laurel	inspires insight and inspiration
mint	stimulates mentally
cedar	reduces fearfulness
peppermint	inspires creativity, attentiveness
pear	grounds and steadies
orange	produces optimism, adaptability
sandalwood	inspires unity and stillness
eucalyptus	encourages openness; clarifies
geranium	increases receptivity and security
grapefruit	revives; lightens
jasmine	heightens harmony and desire
ylang ylang	produces euphoria; sensualizes

FIVE ELEMENTS

Everything in our physical world is composed of one or a combination of three categories of materials. Look around and see if you don't agree that all your material possessions are made from earth, metal, or things that grow (in feng shui we call this element *wood*). Even plastics fall into these categories, deriving from either an earth or a metal source. The remaining two elements, fire and water, are the catalysts that shape all content. (For example, heat bakes earth and permits metal to be manipulated; water can shape through steam or may be an integral ingredient, as with clay.)

Each element communicates, and each element can be described through color, sound, texture, direction, and scent. Thus if you need fire's force—excitement, energy, and intellectual stimulation—you can add the color red or orange; a strong, single sound like a crashing cymbal; a rough texture; a southern exposure; and a peppery, highly charged scent like peppercorns to an environment. The following chart describes the personality of each element and the ways the element expresses itself in our physical world.

Ba-Gua

The ba-gua is a feng shui tool used to explain how different segments of a space are aligned with different emotional messages. The ba-gua divides a space into nine areas, eight sections surrounding the center one. Although you may have seen the ba-gua pictured in an octagonal shape, we use a square shape in this book, for it is closer to the real shape of most rooms and the way we perceive space.

Element	Shape	Color	Texture	Direction	Smell	Sound	Season
fire	triangle	red	rough	south	bitter	cymbals	summer
earth	square	terra-cotta	firm	center	floral musk sweet	drums	May September
metal	circle	reflective white gold silver copper	smooth	west	acrid slippery	xylophone piano	fall
water	wavy lines	black blue	open weave	north	ethereal	harp violin	winter
wood	rectangle	green	grainy	east	minty resinous	reeds horns	spring

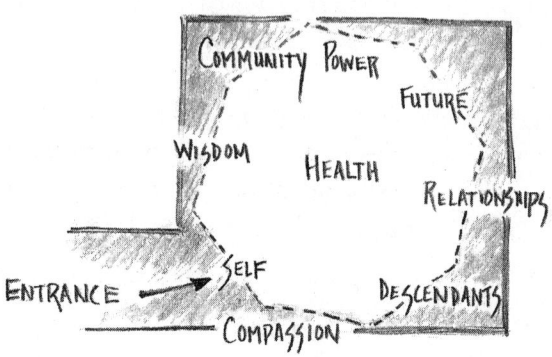

The ba-gua locates where emotional areas exist in any enclosed space.

To understand the specific effect a room has on your experience, overlay the ba-gua on each room. Understanding your home room by room can promote change better than overlaying the ba-gua over an entire dwelling, because each of us experiences most intensely the spaces we are in—not necessarily the spaces outside our immediate experience.

To overlay the ba-gua on a space, imagine that the self side of the ba-gua shown in the diagram is attached to the front of your toes as you stand at the most-used entrance to an area. If for example, you enter a space through a hallway, wait until you reach the area where the entire room is seen and then apply the ba-gua.

BA-GUA AREAS

Each of the nine areas of the ba-gua relate to specific emotional energies. Knowing what emotional messages are underscored by these spaces can help you in choosing seating, artwork, or colors for them. For example, in the future area of a room (the wall area most distant from the entrance) artwork should in some way communicate your goals, desires, and dreams for the future. Thus, a serene pastoral scene is more akin to a stress-free future than a turbulent seascape.

Self Area

The area surrounding the entrance is the area of self. We see spaces from the vantage point of our height, our eyesight, and our preconceived notions or preoccupations. It is in this spot that we subconsciously define how we feel in a space.

What is placed in the self area reflects how we feel about ourselves and how we want others to perceive us.

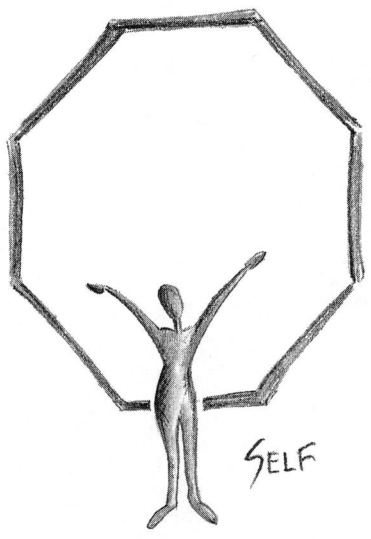

The self area of the ba-gua is positioned at the most frequently used entrance of a room or area. The self area influences your first impression of a space and how you feel while in it.

Compassion Area

The compassion area is directly to the right of the threshold and relates to the way we interact with others. Those not familiar with a space will hesitate and lean to the right, so whoever has control over the space can create either an inhospitable or a welcoming environment for those who enter.

What is placed in the compassion area reflects how we feel about others.

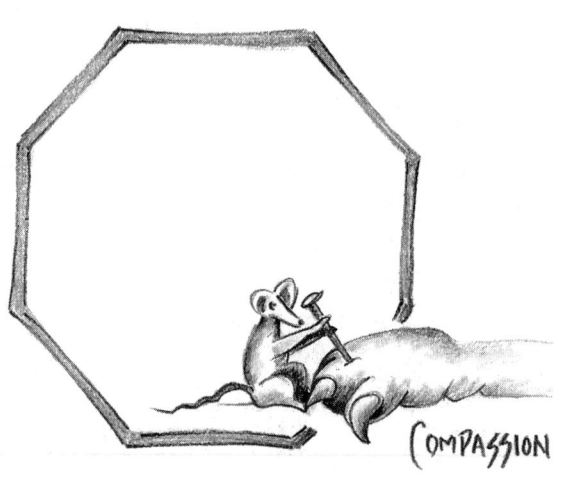

The compassion area defines how you treat others and consequently how you are likely to be treated by others.

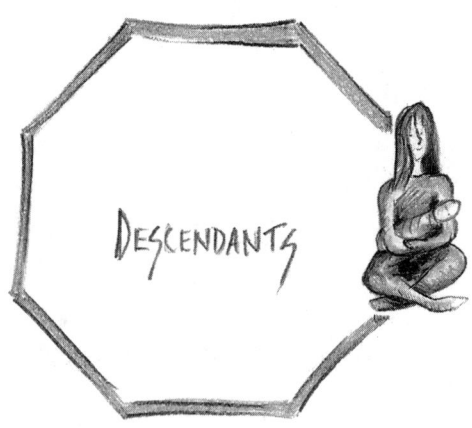

The descendants area reveals what legacy you aspire to create.

Descendants Area

We are biologically programmed to do what it takes to pass our genes on to the next generation. Thus our legacies are an integral part of our consciousness. Our descendants may be our biological children or people whose lives we have influenced in important ways; or they can be our deeds—what we have thought, taught, written, built, or created.

What is placed in the descendants area reflects that which is a valued legacy.

Relationship Area

Tucked away against the far right side, the relationship area is aligned with our most important human connections. Love and its emotional benefits are desired components for a life of contentment.

What is placed in the relationship area reveals our capacity for love and intimacy and promotes or detracts from existing relationships.

The relationship area reveals and influences the strength of your important relationships.

Future Area

The future is positioned in the center wall farthest from the point of entry or self area. We proceed in time from the present to the future.

Our desires for the future are reflected and reinforced by what is placed in this area.

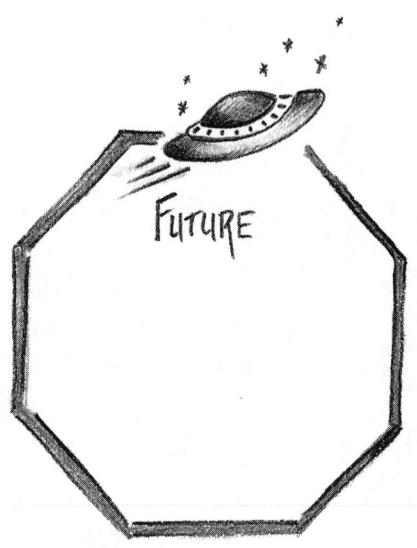

The future area makes public what influences your destiny.

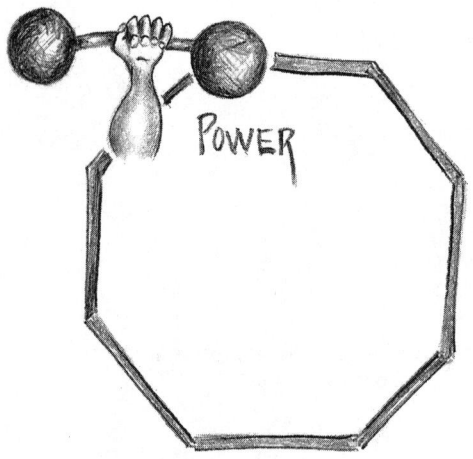

How effective and successful you are is influenced by what is located in the power area of a room.

Power Area

The corner farthest from the door and to the left is associated with power. This area not only reveals whether you feel empowered but also can further your desire to use your personal gifts.

What is placed there mirrors what you wish to augment in life.

Community Area

The notion of community encompasses all those who have influenced you throughout life. From family members to schoolteachers to coworkers and friends, your community is fluid and ever expanding.

What is placed in the community area should demonstrate that you value the best from your past. Do not dwell on what might have been absent or challenging.

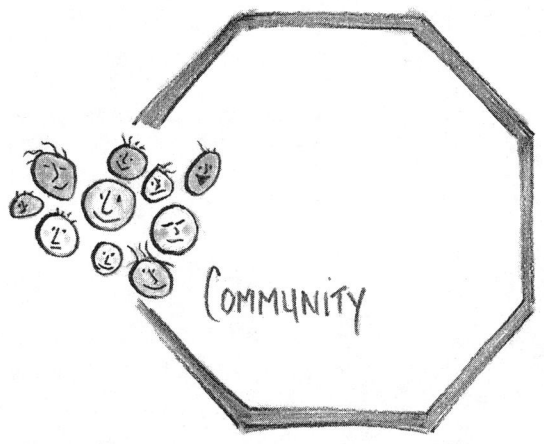

The influences of people and experiences that shaped your life are revealed in the community area.

Wisdom Area

Wisdom, harder to achieve than knowledge, is essential if we are to stay on the path to rewarding, positive lives. There is wisdom of the body, the intellect, and the heart. Everything we do should emanate from wisdom, not rash emotion, manipulation, neurotic impulse, or simply intellectual process.

What is placed in the wisdom area reflects our capacity to negotiate successfully through life.

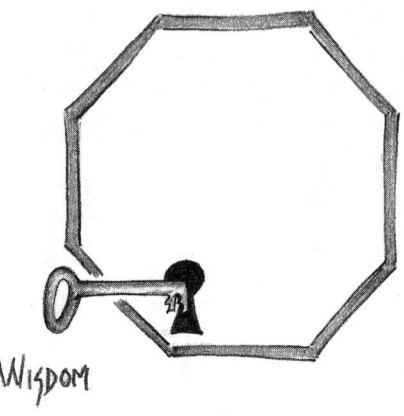

The skills to acquire what is needed to thrive are expressed in the wisdom area.

Health Area

Central to all life experience is our capacity to function and benefit from life. Without health, all else dims. Living without physical, mental, and emotional soundness makes life harder and less fulfilling. Health is central to our lives and to our spaces, from our homes to our cities to our nations.

Your physical, emotional, and spiritual health are exposed by what is placed in the health area.

Emptiness in the center of a room—whether of items, patterns, color, or light—can bespeak a lack of vitality in either our physical, mental, or emotional health.

The ba-gua is a supplementary tool that deepens feng shui's effects. While this book is not designed to teach you to become a feng shui practitioner, knowledge of feng shui's basic tools will give you a deeper understanding of how the cures in the following chapters generate change.

2

Ways to Reduce Sadness and Despondency

There are many gradations of sadness. You may experience a lack of energy, self-doubt, or even bouts of explosive anger that may be signposts of depression or despondency. While feng shui cannot cure clinical depression or other disorders, it can reduce their intensity or provide an avenue for their reversal. Should sadness and despondency persist for an extended period, please seek medical help.

1. What colors cheer?

Red, green, and yellow

What we see accounts for 70 percent of what we process mentally. Therefore color is a principal medium for communication. Unless there is an organic reason for your feelings of depression, you can use color to alleviate gloom and despondency. In nature, colors are aligned appropriately with a message relevant to the source. For example, we perceive the sun as yellow. Because of this association, yellow communicates brightness. Sunlight produces a feel-good hormone, which allows us to equate yellow with optimism. The colors red, green, and yellow transmit messages that are uplifting.

By applying red, yellow, or green fabric to the wall behind a bathroom sink, you will begin your day doused in optimism.

Red

Red is the most prevalent flower color for a good reason. Bright red flowers are meant to stimulate excitement and action in the birds that are needed to pollinate them, for example. Since red has the longest wavelength in the spectrum, it literally jumps out at us, placing itself in front of any other color in our perception. Thus stimulation, excitement, and a call to action—the very antithesis of remaining down in the dumps—are inherent in the color red's message.

Green

Chlorophyll, the pigment that gives most plants their color, is green. Chlorophyll contains the enzyme that is a powerful catalyst for growth and development. When the amount of chlorophyll generated from photosynthesis decreases because of seasonally diminishing light, the plant

A red, green, or yellow starburst hung in a window instills optimism
and inspires a get-up-and-go attitude.

begins to die. In fact leaves don't usually fall to the ground until completely devoid of the color green. Green signals growth and renewal and is a necessary stimulant to the spirit.

Yellow

Scientists have long known that light increases optimism. Because the sun is perceived as yellow and incandescent light glows with a yellow tone, this color exudes the characteristics of light, lending optimism and clarity that are necessary emotional ingredients to feeling upbeat. Using yellow indoors imbues our habitat with cheer and joyfulness.

Suggested Cures

• Cover your bathroom mirror with a fabric of predominantly light green, red, or yellow on a white background. (Yes, there can be other colors, but not to exceed more than 25 percent of the total design.) Install a small makeup/shaving mirror with an accordion arm alongside the covered mirror to service practical needs.

• Place yellow or red flowers, either fresh or silk, in a red vase in a prominent place in your bedroom, living room, study, or kitchen.

• Cut out a red, green, or yellow starburst design in felt, then mount it on fishing line from a dowel. Hang it inside a window you typically look out of when at home, like the one across from your dining room chair.

2. What patterns generate optimism?

Chevrons, diamond shapes, and triangles

Colors are seen within a pattern. A plant leaf may end in a triangular point; the sun is round; a cloud may take on an amorphous, amoebalike shape and a tree trunk the form of a rectangle. Patterns make messages known to us in the same way as colors and have the capacity to com-

Chevrons, triangles, and diamond shapes stimulate energy that
can override depression.

municate what we wish for. Chevrons, diamonds, and triangles communicate optimism and cheer and inspire us to be upbeat.

Any shape with an angle of less than ninety degrees elicits a keener,
more incisive response than do open-angled and rounded objects. Flames
fill the atmosphere with searing energy, as does the slightly haughty green
pine tree when it pierces a winter landscape. Triangles send a message of
transcending their environs, the flame by destroying or burning whatever is available, the pine tree by surviving the cold. In the same way,
chevron shapes elicit a feeling of transcendence over what is.

Suggested Cures

• Hang a square mirror diagonally on a wall that you see frequently.

• Afghans often have a chevron pattern. Drape one that has at least
one dominant red, green, or yellow color over the back of a sofa or at
the foot of your bed.

• Arrange accessories on low tables in groups of three in an overall
triangle.

3. What pattern encourages you to discard habitual ways of thinking and acquire new ones?

Stripes

To override depression you need to feel that new possibilities are before you. One way to uncover such possibilities is to strengthen your belief that you can convert what is into what is wanted.

Change is inherent in all things. Even a rock, seen as immutable, changes over time. In nature change is always accompanied by growth. To promote internal changes, which are at the heart of relieving depression in many cases, you must surround yourself with the characteristics

A striped place setting can release entrenched old habits and be the catalyst to acquiring new healthier ones.

of change. Since all vegetation grows upward or outward, the rectangular line is the shape associated with both change and growth. Vertical lines take precedence over horizontal ones because we associate growth with vertical progress more frequently than horizontal progress.

Therefore using vertical lines and stripes and caring for plants are ways of infusing the energy of change into your environment.

Suggested Cures

• Acquire some fast-growing plants (three is a good number) with long leaves and place them in the areas of your home where you typically sit down. Not only do plants have the benefit of the color green (see Question 1), they also show off their vertical lines. In fact plants have a triple effect on the psyche through color, line, and light. Should you find that the light where you frequently sit down is insufficient, move the chair closer to a light source so that you and the plant can thrive. Living with and tending plants can trigger feelings that overcome sadness.

• Purchase a special place setting for yourself consisting of a striped napkin, place mat, drinking glass, plate, and vase. Use them daily and keep leaves from your plants on the table in the striped vase.

• Acquire some striped fabrics and fold them over existing throw pillows or use them as armrests.

4. What is the simplest change to make in a home to combat common depression?

Light

It is a known fact that being outside on a bright sunny day enhances a sense of well-being. Indeed light is life-giving and acts as a powerful mood elevator. In his book *Light: Medicine of the Future*, scientist Jacob Liberman writes that light affects every organ in our bodies. Without light, he suggests, we would literally wither away and die.

In *The Power of Place*, Winifred Gallagher describes a recent study that found that the rate of depression among native Alaskans was much lower than among transplanted settlers. The study discovered that the single factor contributing to native Alaskans' low incidence of depression is the fact that they traditionally spend as much time as possible outside during winter's diminished daylight hours. In place of the common workday schedule that allows one hour for lunch and perhaps time for a brief walk outside, native Alaskans make optimum use of natural light for games and activities outdoors during the day's brief, light-filled times.

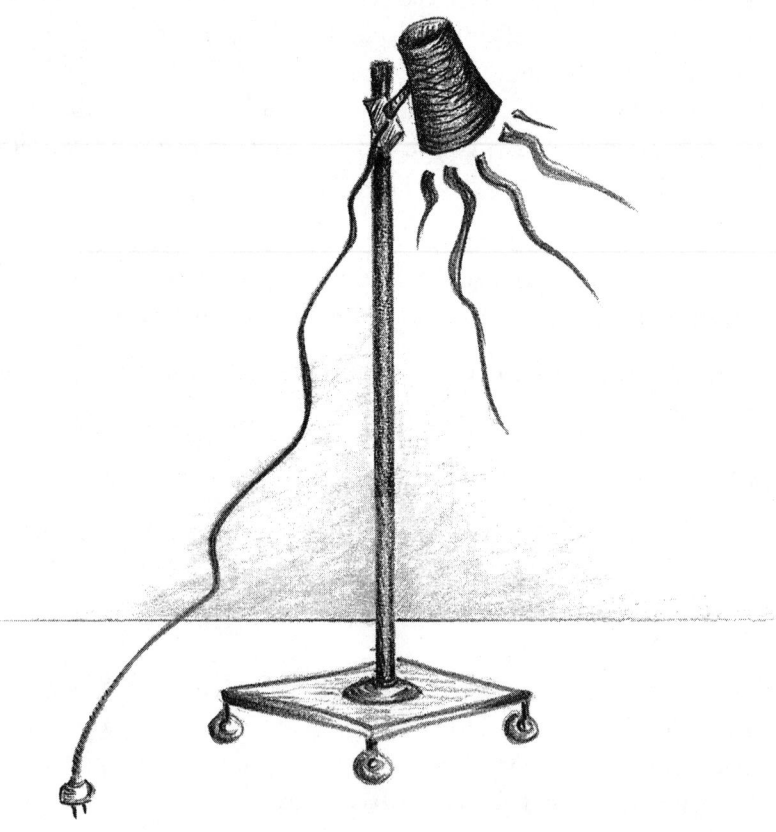

Assemble a portable lamp with a grow light to help you overcome the blues.

Suggested Cures

• Purchase a grow light either in a pet supply store (they are used on fish tanks) or at a gardening supply center and mount it on a simple rolling device much like the IV stands that allow hospital patients to walk about. Since it will be portable, you can use it while working at your desk or reading in a chair or in any space where you spend more than half an hour at a time. The recommended minimum use is four hours a day. Should the construction of a mobile device exceed your carpentry capabilities, try using a simple desk lamp with a grow light in exactly the same way. Move it along with you from task to task.

• Take mini-walks outdoors during daylight hours. Aim for ten minutes three times a day. If you find you're not motivated to get outside without a "good" reason, place bird feeders along your route that will need to be filled, walk your own dog or a neighbor's, or move your mailbox away from the front door.

• Move the kitchen table, your desk, or any frequently used chair near a south- or east-facing window.

5. What is a simple way to invigorate and enliven an environment?

A fan

One of the deficiencies of indoor space is the near total lack of air movement. Breezes and air currents counteract a sense of dullness and loneliness. Since our skin is our largest receptacle for sensory stimulation, the lack of air movement measurably adds to the sense of isolation that is so prevalent in those who feel depressed. Action will generate reaction, and an environment that changes and literally exhales stimulation invigorates us.

Suggested Cure

Set up small tabletop fans operated by timers throughout your home. Point each at objects that will respond with movement, such as a plant,

Position a fan on a plant. Movement brings emotional buoyancy
to a still setting.

so that you not only feel the breeze as you pass by but also see and hear
the rustling of the object. Put one fan facing the foot of the bed and set
it to start blowing twenty minutes before your alarm goes off. The subtle flutter of your bed linens will energize the waking process. Put another
in the kitchen, set to start blowing across a moveable object just before
you're likely to enter to prepare the most time-consuming meal of the
day. Have a foyer fan activated at the time when you're likely to be returning home from work and put one in the room you tend to occupy during the hours of 3:00 to 5:00 P.M. Finally, after dinner, set a fan to run
for one and a half hours in your gathering space.

6. What TV station can make you feel less isolated?

The Weather Channel

For people whose depression is magnified when they spend time alone, adding human voices to their surroundings can help. Too often regular programming carries the unnatural sound of canned laughter or is interrupted by noisy commercials. While TV watching may suppress negative feelings and provide some comfort as a substitute for companionship, it is a passive pastime that rarely inspires people to initiate the activities that alleviate many forms of depression. Therefore listening to voices that do not entice you to watch the TV screen is a good way to fill the silence and feel the comfort of companionship while staying engaged elsewhere.

The weather stations' regular changes of announcers fill the home with a medley of pleasant male and female voices throughout the day, devoid of the suspense-building dialogue that would invite listeners to focus on what is said.

Suggested Cure

Tune your TV set to a weather channel whenever you feel alone or lonely.

The weather channel broadcasts with a variety of voices in intervals that
can lessen the sense of loneliness.

7. What textures stimulate and spur you to action?

Textures associated with a positive memory and textures with a distinct feel

In the same way a towel rubbed across your back after a luxurious bath promotes circulation, a firm surface underfoot provides stability, and silk against the skin creates a sense of coolness, all textures arouse emotions.

What fabrics do you particularly delight in? Do freshly laundered and newly ironed bedsheets make you feel taken care of? Does the open weave of a doily on a sofa's arm remind you of a favorite relative? Does the pull of a sticky plastic chair seat on the back of your leg catapult you back to a summer camp's arts and crafts program? For all of us certain textures are associated with positive memories. What textures can you replicate that transport you back in time to pleasant events of the past?

If evoking memories is difficult for you, then consider some generic conditions from the cures that follow.

Suggested Cures

Select a texture and a location from the following table that best suit your situation.

Texture	What It Evokes	Where You Might Position It
silky	being soothed or refreshed	pillowcase, a throw on a sofa
pile	stimulation, responsiveness	area rugs at threshold of rooms, towels
velvet	luxury, exotic experiences	throw pillows on sofa, lap cover
coarse	action, motivation	desktop pad, rattan bath mat
open weave	opportunity, choice	curtains, place mats

8. What aromas stimulate action?

Fire scents

Scents provoke a whole range of emotional, intellectual, and physical reactions. When you need a kick-start to alter patterns of behavior that are not furthering your contentment, the scents associated with fire can do the trick. Feng shui divides all things into five elemental groups—fire, earth, metal, water, and wood. Each element has a personality, and all things classified in one of the five elements acquire that element's personality. The fire element stimulates action and reaction.

When depressed, you may experience fatigue and depletion of energy, in which case the fire element scent is the appropriate one to breathe into the atmosphere.

Suggested Cures

- The following aromas are categorized as fire element:

Lemon
Melissa
Rose
Jasmine
Ginger

Ginger, lemon, and rosemary are three scents that stimulate and energize.

Laurel
Rosemary
Tea Tree

Before selecting a scent, go to a store that carries a large selection of essential oils and smell each one. Each person has preferences based on past experiences with smell, and many times a particular scent will stimulate specific positive or negative memories. Choose a scent that feels right to you.

• Your chosen scent should be used in small doses and repeated often. Because there is an enzyme in our nose that obscures a scent after a very short period of time, you need to keep inhaling a scent over and over again. The best way to use the scent is to inhale it directly from the bottle or from a drenched cotton ball. Keep it close by. If, for example, you spend time writing or talking on the telephone, breathe the scent in every time you pick up a pen or the phone. Direct contact with the scent gives the best results.

The physical environment can be a healing aid for depression that does not have an organic reason. Sadness and despondency are generally yin conditions whose grip is hard to disengage from. The cures suggested here are mostly yang, designed to promote the stimulus needed to prevent or release sadness.

3

Ways to Reduce Stress

S tress can be defined as a condition of tension that is produced by relationship problems, unrealistically high expectations, too-busy lives, or deprivation. Today stress is epidemic in our daily lives as people become wound tighter and tighter. Stress can manifest itself as a self-destructive habit, a short temper, a physical condition, or a general feeling of unhappiness. All of the ideas in this chapter can be beneficial on some level in relieving stress.

9. What category of sounds dissipates stress?

The diversity of nature's voices

Throughout most of human history we lived as hunter/gatherers or agrarians, and our waking hours were spent outdoors. Our senses evolved to allow us to survey our surroundings so we could protect ourselves from threats as well as take full advantage of nature's bounty. We are still programmed deeply to want to hear the sounds of our surroundings. Being cut off from the intermittent sounds of the natural world leads our subconscious attention to our vulnerability.

An atmosphere without natural sounds makes us feel not only exposed but also isolated. We are meant to be in community with others in an animate environment. When we are instead isolated, we feel stress. Stress can, therefore, be viewed as an outgrowth of sensory deprivation.

The sights and sounds of the natural world are so deeply ingrained in us that most of us feel more alive when outside listening to the songs of birds, the rustle of leaves blown in the wind, and the trickling of waters over the rock and earth. When separated in silence or sequestered artificially with sounds unrelated to nature such as the mechanical whine of heating or air-conditioning, the hum of machinery, or the noise of passing traffic, we often lose the sense of ease and the calming effect that nature so readily provides.

A clock that chimes bird calls brings nature's sounds inside and generates a sense of well-being.

Suggested Cures

• Select a tape or CD that uses nature as its instruments. Your local music or New Age store will be able to make current suggestions. As I write this book, I like Dan Gibson's Solitudes, Volume One, *Canoe to Loon Lake/Dawn by a Gentle Stream* (produced and copyrighted by Dan Gibson's Productions for Eddie Bauer, Redmond, WA, manufactured and distributed by Holborne Distributing Co., Mount Albert, Ontario), which focuses on the pleasures of water flowing soothingly over rocks and around outstretching logs and branches. Play the sounds of nature twice a day, once in the morning when you wake up to set a tone of harmony for the day and again between 4:00 and 6:00 P.M. or at the end of the workday and the beginning of personal evening time.

• Purchase a clock that chimes with birdcalls on the hour.

• Add a water feature in a room used for relaxation.

• Position a fan on an indoor plant to hear the sounds of its leaves rustling.

10. What scene and color lowers blood pressure?

Medium tone of blue or the color of water

Human beings start life floating in liquid for nine months. In a healthy womb environment the fetus is provided for perfectly. Thus we have on the most primal level an association with water that is reflected in balance and harmony.

Scientists have conducted experiments and determined that the color blue can lower blood pressure and reduce stress reactions. The color blue is the color of self, encouraging those who view it to become introspective and pensive. Therefore either being enfolded in a water scene or contemplating the color of blue water can be a trigger for eliminating the feeling of stress.

Hang a picture with a calm scene to reduce stress in areas where
you tend to be tense.

Suggested Cures

• Hang a picture of a calm seascape, especially in an environment that
generates stress.

• Paint a room light blue.

• Drape a blue comforter over a chair or sofa facing you in a room
you typically spend time in.

• Create a screen from material called foam core, which is lightweight
and easily scored. After scoring it, sponge-paint it in colors of blue and
position it to hide stimulating colors or to hide from view stimulating
scenes such as a work area or a busy street.

11. What color can reduce feelings of frenzy?

Pink (call it salmon *or* adobe *if* pink *sounds overly feminine)*

After World War II, the U.S. Navy supported research to determine whether color deflects aggressive behavior. The study recorded the different reactions of detainees at a juvenile facility, who were typically highly charged, when moved to a holding room. The room had been successively painted different colors. Green, normally associated with vegetation and the outdoors, was tried first, but it did not change behavior. Neither did blue, yellow, or white. However, the final color, pink, evoked some remarkable reactions. In fact, after twenty minutes in the pink holding room a statistically significant number of young men fell asleep. Pink, it appears, promotes a relaxed state even in a milieu of tension.

Suggested Cures

Use pink to subdue stressful conditions:

- Can't sit still and relax? Paint the room you spend the most time in a salmon shade.

- Difficulty falling asleep? Paint the ceiling of your bedroom a pink tone, such as salmon, adobe, or coral.

- Too much hysteria when your family gathers together? Use salmon tones for matting pictures hung in your family's gathering rooms and place a few rose-toned lightbulbs in lamps throughout the room.

- Family argues at the dinner table? Use a bouquet of muted-pink flowers as the dining table's centerpiece or a tablecloth or place mats in pink tones.

12. What colors should you avoid when stressed out?

Red and green in combination

Like a rubber band stretched to the point of snapping, stress taxes our system until we reach the breaking point and become incapable of handling the situations we encounter appropriately. Since 70 percent of our information about the world is taken in through our eyes, colors inevitably greatly influence our daily experience.

Objects in nature are colored so that their innate energy matches the life force they exude. For example, the downside of the fire element's color, red, is that it is volatile, explosive, and potentially threatening. The color green stimulates growth and change, which when attached to the negative side of red can convey and evoke continued excitement, action, and reaction—hardly a beneficial message when a sense of calm is called for.

Suggested Cures

• If there are fabrics or walls in reds and greens in your home and you don't want to re-cover, repaint, or remove, add yellow. Yellow will override or mitigate the jarring message of combined red and green to make it more manageable. Yellow counteracts intensity by adding the message of enlightenment and optimism.

• Add yellow by placing yellow throw pillows on a green and red sofa.

• Place a vase filled with yellow flowers against red and green wallpaper.

13. What patterns intensify stress?

Triangles, diamonds, and chevrons

Second to color as potential stress factors in an environment are shapes. Just like colors (see Question 12), all shapes take on the personality of

Pictures with dominant triangular shapes are stressful and should be moved
from view when relaxation is required.

the forms they are connected with in nature. However, different emotional states react to shapes and color in different ways.

Consider the shape of a flame, a triangle. When you are depressed, this shape spurs you to action, but when you are stressed you are likely to experience the challenging side of the shape. The fire shape, a triangle can be challenging to those who are stressed exactly because it spurs them to action at a time when they need calming. Triangles, pyramids, chevrons, and diamonds are all unsettling shapes when stressed and should be avoided.

Suggested Cures

• Carefully go through your home and remove any sets of three items that you find. Three suggests a triangle.

• Remove any paintings in prominent places that include triangles, chevrons, and diamond patterns.

14. What types of lighting interfere with relaxation?

Ceiling light

Generally one bright light directed from the ceiling is experienced as daytime. Daytime body rhythms are active because it is during the light-filled hours that our species is meant to do the work required to survive. In fact when darkness descends, hormones that actually make us sleepy are released in our body.

Ceiling lights that spread a diffused overall luminosity replicate daytime and actually depress our ability to relax.

Suggested Cures

• Turn off the ceiling lights and use only incandescent light from individual lamps.

• Aim the existing ceiling lights on paintings or a door.

• Purchase a lamp for the room you spend most of your time in that throws a cone of light.

15. What wall color causes tension and should be avoided when stressed?

White

By reflecting back all colors, white actually produces an intensity that can cause stress. When you see a specific color, you experience all of its emotional vocabulary, but with white you are forced to react without being steered in a particular direction. This intensity forces you to explore mentally. White makes you think without taking a break. Obviously, then, you don't want to be surrounded by it when you feel a deep need to relax.

Low-wattage wall or ceiling spots with colored bulbs located every several feet can produce a yin atmosphere, which is conducive to unwinding.

Suggested Cure

If your walls are white and repainting them would be too large a project, purchase one clip-on spotlight for each eight running feet of wall space and a colored lightbulb to wash the wall areas you frequently see with a relaxing color. Here are some choices:

Pink for relaxing before going to sleep
Blue for being able to focus on your needs
Orange to enhance the mind-set to associate with others

16. What is the best overall relaxing aroma?

Lavender

Lavender is overall the best scent to promote peacefulness. However, the trick is to know where to burn or aerate its fragrance.

While scent, like color and shape, has some generic qualities, it is important to consider your own personal experience with a particular scent. Suppose you had a disagreeable, haughty, and overbearing aunt who wore a particular perfume that contained a dominant ingredient like musk. No matter how popular the scent, you would never respond to it in a positive way. So while I suggest lavender as a scent to diffuse, soak in, or wear to help soothe the spirit, body, and mind during certain times of the day, be sure you respond favorably to it before you use it.

Suggested Cures

• Place a scent diffuser on a timer to dispense lavender at the same time as your alarm clock goes off. Instead of waking feeling harried and stressed, you will be eased into the day by this scent.

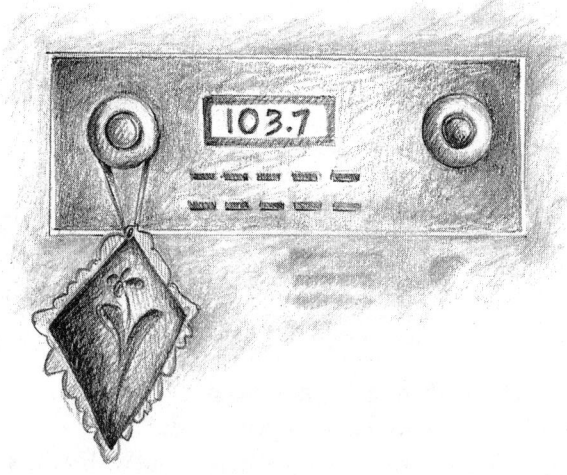

Hang a lavender potpourri during biologically stressful hours, between 3:00 and 6:00 P.M. wherever you are, even in your car.

• During the second stressful period of the day, between 3:00 and 5:00 P.M., when the body runs on empty, we may feel the need to eat or drink to relieve tension and tiredness. Instead, dab lavender oil on the tip of your nose or hang a lavender potpourri in an inconspicuous place in your car so that it distributes its soothing fragrance on the drive home.

• Later on, to set a relaxed tone for the evening, light lavender candles or incense.

• At the end of a particularly stressful day, bathe in lavender flower petals and oils or use lavendar soap.

17. What ambience can assist you in slowing down?

Yin ambience

To subdue feelings of frenzy, it is important to be surrounded with what we, in feng shui, call a *yin state*. Like entering a museum or church, yin atmospheres produce a stillness and sense of serenity. Yin spaces are a breath of calmness and peacefulness. Yin spaces encourage you to unwind and mellow out.

Suggested Cures

Yin applications should be installed in those spaces you use frequently.

Kitchen

• Spot lighting under the cabinets, not overhead.

• If your counter tops are shiny, cover the largest surface with a muted-toned washable runner or chopping surface.

Bedroom

• Toss a muted-colored solid afghan over a brightly colored bedspread.

• Select a light pastel pillowcase to sleep on.

To create a yin or relaxing atmosphere in a kitchen, light the work area underneath the wall cabinets, not from the ceiling. Cover shiny work surfaces with a muted solid such as a large plain wood cutting board.

• Be sure that when you are sitting in bed the opposite wall has a painting or wall covering without high-contrast colors.

Living Room or Gathering Space

• Cover a glass coffee table with a square of muted fabric.

• If changing a room's colors is not an option, keep the room dimly lit or install some colored bulbs to mute the existing colors.

18. What sound helps you feel grounded and centered?

A consistent, even beat

Research shows that when baby monkeys were raised by two kinds of surrogate mothers, the babies whose mother was a chicken wire form wrapped in a towel with a ticking clock inside grew bigger and were less irritable than the babies with a surrogate composed of a chicken wire form wrapped in a towel without a ticking clock. The sole variation was the sound of the clock. This scientific experiment demonstrates that a heartbeatlike sound produces a heightened sense of well-being both physically and mentally.

In utero the first sense fully developed by the fetus is the sense of hearing. It is therefore no wonder that we are deeply soothed by the constancy of a repetitive, regular beat.

Suggested Cures

- Place a ticking clock where it can be heard throughout the home.

- Purchase a water feature that trickles rather than flows.

- Use a metronome in rooms where you want to feel secure and safe.

19. What walkway shapes produce a tranquil state of mind for your return home?

Curved

When water flows on a flat surface, it speeds up as it proceeds. Similarly, when following a straight pathway, we tend to move faster and faster. If the pathway leading to our front door is straight, we are propelled to walk briskly. Stress is often heightened when we are pressed to hasten. The more rushed we feel, the more tense we become. Straight paths are like an annoying stranger pushing you to proceed. Thus it is important to design a curved walkway leading to your home's entrance.

Suggested Cures

If reconstructing a straight pathway is not possible, here's what you can do on its edges to interrupt the straight lines:

- Reshape the edges with potted plants.

- Cut away at the grass and fill with stones that match the walkway's color.

• If the area is large enough, interrupt it with potted plants or beds of vegetation to ensure that you walk in curves.

• If you live in an apartment and have no control over the hallway decor, remember to glance to both the right and the left as you proceed down a straight hallway rather than look straight ahead.

Reshape a straight path to the main entrance by positioning planters and flowers to give the illusion of curves and thereby slow down your physical pace and your mental activity.

4

Ways to Eliminate Insecurity

C ures for boosting self-esteem can benefit almost all of us. Few people don't suffer from feeling inadequate in some area of their lives.
For some, insecurity exists in general areas such as entertaining or decorating; for others lack of confidence endures in more pervasive ways
like speaking their mind, feeling capable at work, or engaging in intimacy. Underpinning most feelings of inadequacy is a lack of self-worth.
Thus, the cures suggested in this chapter focus on building personal
power. Some cures encourage being open and expressive with others,
which helps us feel acknowledged, thus increasing our self-esteem.

Observing the power corner in the ba-gua of your home office, bedroom, or main gathering room can be a good indicator of a need for
increasing self-esteem. A lack of objects reflecting self-worth and personal accomplishment in this area indicates a need for raising your level
of self-confidence.

20. What colors help you focus on your personal strengths?

Blue, purple, and gray

Your self-esteem will skyrocket when you focus on your accumulated personal assets instead of your perceived faults. Children often begin life with a natural feeling of self-worth. It is only when parents start to impose expectations on them that they learn to measure their accomplishments by another's yardstick—and begin to come up wanting. Naturally, very young children need to pay attention to their parents' expectations if they are to learn to navigate a complicated world. But too many of us stop trusting our own judgment altogether and lead lives of self-doubt. When we relearn self-reliance, we return to a focus on the moment and stop wasting time and energy weighing every little decision against the expectations and demands of others.

You can relearn self-reliance by enlisting the aid of the color blue, which allows you to turn inward and focus on the self. Purple plays a role by helping you recognize that there is more to life than others' expectations. Gray stands in between complete reflection of all light and total absorption of all light. In that center, like the fulcrum on which a seesaw's plank rests, there is perfect balance. Surrounding yourself with this balance of color gives you a physical representation of equilibrium allowing you to hear your inner voice.

Suggested Cures

• Paint the door to a room you spend time in either blue, purple, or gray.

• Cover an entire desktop or work surface with gray glass or paint an existing desktop gray.

• Hang blue, purple, or gray fabric from a dowel in front of a frequently used spot.

21. What position in a room increases a sense of power?

The seat facing and farthest away from the entrance door

Imagine living during the cave-dwelling days. Where would you choose to bed down for the night? Would it be the spot closest to the cave entrance? Certainly not. If a prowling tiger happened inside, you would be its first delicacy. Most likely you would choose the location farthest from the entrance. In that position you would have time to react to danger while being protected from the rear by having your back against a wall.

In the same way, royal thrones are placed farthest from the entrance with their backs against the wall. The place in a room that is safest, and therefore most power producing, is at the wall farthest from the threshold. If you choose to locate a desk chair, a reading chair, or any furniture where you spend a large part of your time in that position, you will automatically feel powerful. You will also likely be the first person to be greeted when people enter the space, and being acknowledged bolsters your self-esteem even further.

Suggested Cures

• If you can place your favorite chair farthest from the entrance, against a wall, be sure to signal to guests to take other seats when entering the room.

• If there is no wall at the point farthest from the entrance:

Position a high plant behind a favored
  chair.
Locate a folding screen behind your usual
  seat.
Close the window treatment if there is a
  window behind the chair you use.

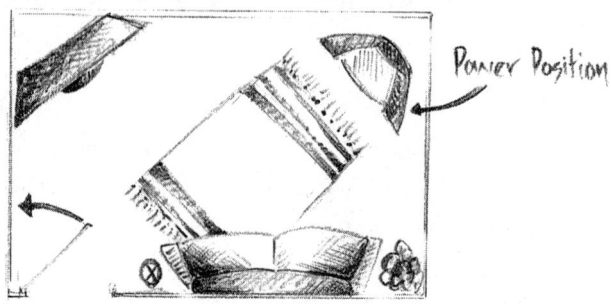

The seat farthest from yet facing the entrance to a gathering room is the power seat.

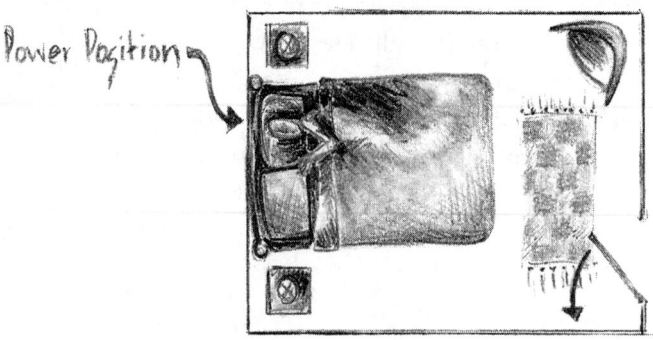

When sleeping alone, the side of the bed farthest from but in view of the bedroom door is the power position.

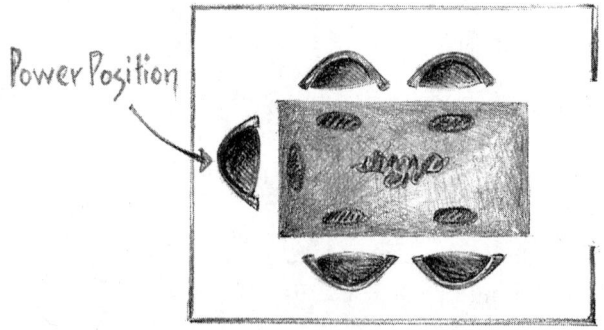

The chair at your dining table that is farthest from yet facing the entrance is the power position.

22. Where in a room should you place representations of personal successes to increase your self-worth?

On the far left side of the room as seen from the entrance

Instinctively most people move to or turn to the right when entering a space. Therefore the left side of a room represents challenges or the roads least traveled. Coupled with the far side, it can be viewed as the area promoting the most personal power. In feng shui, in fact, we call the far left side of a room the *self-empowerment* or *power area*. By placing symbols of past accomplishments and realized goals, you set the ball rolling toward feeling your power.

Suggested Cures

On the far left side of a room, place:

- pictures of desired personal goals

- plaques or awards

- a photograph of an accomplishment

- items made from metal

- artwork with a predominance of red, orange, or gold

Your self-esteem skyrockets when a representation of successes hangs in the power area of a frequently used room.

23. What colors inspire you to share your feelings and ideas when dining?

Red, orange, green, and blue

Mealtimes, especially dinnertime, are often the only times of day when family members take the time to sit down and converse. Therefore, how you communicate at the dinner table, whether at home or elsewhere, contributes greatly to how others experience you. When you don't feel acknowledged or understood, self-esteem and, thus, satisfaction plummet.

Red, green, blue, and orange ribbons hanging in combination or individually from a light can inspire conversation.

What faces you directly when you sit at the dinner table has a significant impact on how confidently you handle conversations. The colors red and orange stimulate responding. At the same time, overstimulation may make you feel nervous or talk for the sake of talking; therefore, what you see should be balanced by green or blue.

Green, the color that unlocks the desire for knowledge, and blue, the color of self-confidence, are the perfect accompaniments to red and orange. While this may seem like a tall order, you will be surprised to discover just how many posters, pictures, and calendars contain a combination of these colors.

Suggested Cures

If you don't have an appropriate piece of art at hand, position green, blue, red, and orange in your sight line while dining by:

- placing red, orange, green, and blue vases on a shelf or windowsill facing your seat

- using green/blue and red/orange place mats and dishes

- hanging a mobile containing these colors

- attaching ribbons with these colors from a lamp or ceiling fixture

24. What color tones are good for building self-esteem?

Bright, light, and vibrant

Maybe you remember the high school experience of waiting for someone to ask you to dance or anxiously listening for your name to be called among those who had made a team. Being noticed and acknowledged is a surefire way of gaining self-assurance and feeling appreciated. Even if you are not naturally outgoing, you can accomplish this by placing yourself in an attention-getting setting.

A male friend of mine who had raised four children alone once attended a school soccer game and noticed a woman sitting alone on a red blanket watching her son's match. The rest is, as the saying goes, history. After the red blanket had caught his attention, he mustered up enough courage to go to her side and make a casual remark. Had she not been surrounded by red, who knows if they would have met?

Suggested Cures

- At the office or at home in the dining room, hang a poster or a piece of fabric with sharply contrasting bright colors behind your seat.

- If you are not at home, try to:

    Sit in front of a solid-colored wall.
    Sit down on a light-colored or brightly upholstered piece of furniture.
    Stand in front of a vibrant painting.

25. Which door should you enter when returning home?

The main entrance

If you routinely return home through the front door, rather than the garage, back, or side door, your relation to home and family will be enriched and your self-worth boosted. As a rule, the front door has a larger and more impressive pathway, and both the landing and the door tend to be more decorative than the other entrances to your home. Moreover, once inside, a front entrance is usually assigned an architectural power view. Since it is the first view of home, the statement it makes about a home and those who live there has a strong, if only subconscious, impact. Finally, a front entrance is designed for transitions. It might typically contain a foyer table and open up to a main space such as the gathering room. Like all first impressions, the entrance sets the tone for all subsequent experience. Giving yourself the chance to switch from work mode to family mode and looking forward to gathering with those you love—or just relaxing on your own—does a lot more for your feelings of self-worth than entering directly into the kitchen or laundry room, as if your role at home is cooking or cleaning.

Suggested Cures

- Clear a pathway to the main entrance from the location where you customarily park your car.

- Place an object close to the front door that you typically have to interact with, such as a box of birdseed on the path to the front door. This might encourage you to pass that way intentionally so as to fill the bird feeder.

- Place a mail receptacle by the front door.

- Place other enticements near the front door, such as:

Aromatic plants
A flower-covered trellis
A chair to sit on while removing boots or shoes prior to entering
   the house

Create a pleasant task that will lure you to use your front door, such as using a
birdseed bin for filling a bird feeder. Using a front door boosts self-esteem.

26. What sound and touch combination is likely to strengthen a positive sense of self?

Your own footsteps on the floor

Have you ever hummed a tune while concentrating on a mental task? Do you find it comforting to stroke your arm, pull an ear, or scratch your head in your quest for new ideas? Touch and sound can soothe us.

Steady footsteps, like the swinging pendulum of a grandfather clock, replicate a heartbeat and comfort us on a primal level. Creating an environment that naturally invites us to walk unimpeded for at least four or five steps over a surface that will reverberate with our footsteps will complement other supportive choices.

Reflexologists understand that the feet are important for total body stimulation. The nerve endings of each organ end in specific points on the bottom of our feet. Applying pressure to the bottom of the feet stimulates all the organs of the body. What does this have to do with raising self-esteem? When we care for ourselves, we implicitly acknowledge our own worth.

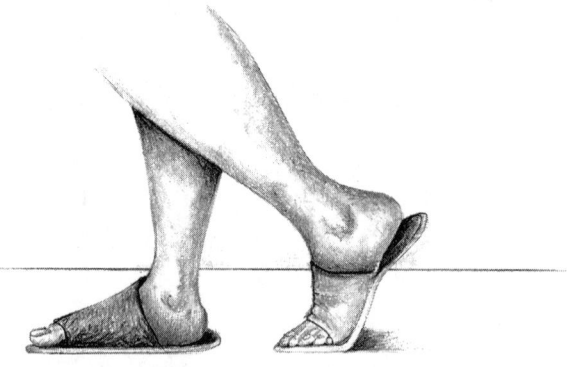

Your own footsteps can strengthen self-esteem because they generate sound and touch, which are both needed to feel vital.

Suggested Cures

- Clear a pathway inside your home that feels natural to walk along for a minimum of four or five normal strides.

- Walk barefoot or with thin-soled house shoes or slippers to enhance stimulation.

- Have a well-traveled hallway or part of a room stripped of carpet.

27. What lighting interferes with self-worth?

Any lamp that casts the edge of its shadow across you when you're seated

Notice that when you're with a group of people you often observe first those who are encircled by the most intense light. While the eye is an exceedingly complex mechanism, it is guided by a rather simple set of

Remove any light that casts a shadow on a seated person. Having a shadow cast across your body reduces your authority and undermines self-worth.

criteria, and intensity of light is primary among them. When a shadow is cast across your body, the place where light and dark meet forces the eyes to track what is inside the brightest area. Visually, this cuts you in two and detracts from a sense of your wholeness. In the same way as a spotlight highlights the person inside its narrow periphery, being in the center of a circle of light commands attention. When you get attention, your self-worth is increased.

Suggested Cures

• Make sure the lamps next to your seating areas are tall enough to cast light over the entire person, whether on a chair or sofa. If you don't want to purchase new lights, raise the ones you have on an interesting box, stand, or object.

• Reposition your chair or seating area under unbroken light.

28. What scents build confidence?

Lemon, laurel, and rosemary

If you have ever felt frustrated by the inability to come up with an idea that was on the tip of your tongue, or you've missed an opportunity because you were at a loss for words, then you know you'd feel more confident if you were able to access your thoughts in time to make appropriate and quick responses. Like the creative process, epiphanies and intuitive brilliance don't have to be muscled into action. Ideas always smolder below the surface of consciousness until, like a buoy at sea, they suddenly appear to guide the way.

The unconscious mind can be likened to the ocean, with our consciousness a lone boat atop its vast expanse. Scents can be used to signal the unconscious. When they do so, all you need to do is be ready and receptive to the currents of thoughts rising to the surface. Knowing that is possible is a real confidence builder.

Suggested Cures

• *Lemon*: When the mind becomes congested with obsessive or negative thoughts, lemon unclogs it. Lemon is associated with cleanliness and therefore is a clarifier. Like its color, yellow, lemon is the scent of acuity, which clears confusion and separates the substantive from the unessential. Lemon enhances learning of facts or figures.

• *Laurel*: Laurel is a mood enhancer and an aid to concentration and memory. It can aid those who lack confidence by stimulating creative boldness. For those who doubt their insights and are self-limiting, laurel can increase the capacity for intuition.

• *Rosemary*: For centuries this herb has been associated with strengthening a weak memory. This confidence builder empowers the mind and reinforces the power of emotional knowingness.

29. What seating position erodes power?

Seats in front of a window or an open door

Because our sense of self-preservation keeps us attuned to modifications in our environment, movement beyond a window and a distant view can divert the attention of even the most focused person. Sitting with your back to a window encourages others to look past you. Not being paid attention to enervates us and weakens self-esteem.

Suggested Cures

• Try not to sit with a window or a door directly behind you.

• Should there be no alternative, here are some remedies to employ:

Place a plant higher than your head behind you.
Purchase a high-backed chair.

Install a shade or a half-curtain that can be pulled up to others' eye-level so that light can come in but people looking at you can't see out.

Keep the door closed when one is positioned behind your chair.

Locate a folding screen directly behind your chair.

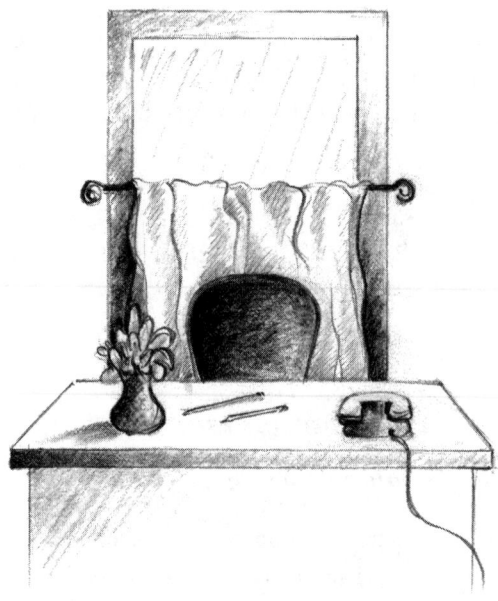

A half-curtain behind a chair in front of a window can provide a continuous background and bolster your authority, and are therefore empowering.

5

Ways to Win at Weight Management

The current upswing in obesity in the United States is alarming. Excess body fat can impact physical and psychological health. Being overweight often causes anxiety and low self-esteem. Repeated unsuccessful attempts to alter eating patterns can promote feelings of failure, trigger depression, and prevent people from tapping into their strengths. While we know that nutritional soundness and regular exercise are essential to losing weight, an often under-considered facet is your daily environment. This chapter is designed to be an additional support tool to help you win at the losing game.

30.   What color reduces the pace of eating?

Blue

No savvy fast-food chain uses the color blue in its restaurant decor, because blue slows down the pace of eating. Faber Birren, the noted color researcher and author, has documented experiments demonstrating that a room painted blue actually lowers blood pressure and generally diminishes activity levels.

Creating an atmosphere that entices you to slow down will result in your eating less. One common problem for those struggling to lose weight is eating too quickly. It takes the brain about twenty minutes to acknowledge feeling full. When you wolf food down, you don't have enough time to connect with that satiated feeling. All of us who have grabbed a large bag of chips and devoured its contents can attest to that. It feels impossible to stop eating until the whole bag is gone, not because a few chips didn't satisfy hunger but because we have eaten them too quickly.

Suggested Cures

- Integrate blue colors into the dining areas of your home.

- Use blue plates or glasses.

- Decorate the table's center with a blue bowl filled with blue glass beads.

- Hang a serene seascape across from your dining chair.

- Cover the dining table with a blue cloth or place mats.

31.   What color and lines make you eat faster?

Red and diagonal lines

The color red excites and energizes. It also plays a role in quickening your pace. Red sports cars seem jazzier and faster than blue ones. Red in general accelerates an activity. As they say in restaurant vernacular, red turns tables faster than other colors. Almost all fast-food chains make use of the color red in the decor for precisely this reason.

When I moved from New York City to New Jersey, five pounds went on my frame as if by magic. The cause of my newly acquired weight turned out to be the painting that had previously hung over the living room sofa but had been moved to the wall facing my dining table seat! The diagonal lines sweeping the canvas brought even more attention to the dominant red color scheme. The combination of pattern and color was a double whammy. Red in conjunction with diagonal lines is a loud call for a direct response and will increase the likelihood that you will, without awareness, eat faster and consequently more.

Suggested Cures

- Avoid using red napkins, place mats, or tablecloths.

- Don't eat while looking at a red (brick, wood, or paint) wall or flooring.

- Don't use red in wallpaper in rooms where you eat.

- Steer clear of wooden serving pieces with overtones of red, such as mahogany or rosewood.

- Avoid serving food in copper accessories (copper has a reddish tone).

- Don't hang pictures on a wall in a layout that creates a diagonal line.

Eliminate pictures hung in diagonal lines when dieting.

Tie-back curtains create a diagonal shape and undermine conscious/careful eating.

• Untie tie-back curtains.

• Avoid placing tall and small furnishings side by side, as well as arrangements that reproduce a triangle.

• Even when the overall color scheme of a piece of art, wallpaper, or other part of your decor is not red and diagonal lines are not immediately apparent, they are often incorporated in subtle ways. For example, wall art can be hung in a diagonal pattern on the wall or differently sized furnishings positioned next to each other can create a diagonal line. Eliminate as many diagonal lines as possible, especially in your dining area.

A grouping of furnishings positioned so that their overall shape is a triangle is disadvantageous when dieting because it stimulates eating quickly.

32. What colors maximize the appeal of healthy foods at a meal?

Salmon and russet

Optimum weight maintenance is often sabotaged by an improper diet. We fill up on empty calories and then crave more junk because our body knows it needs nutrients! We should be furious with the manufacturers of junk foods, because they trick our bodies with hard-to-resist habit-forming additives and seductive colors. Pink candy, pale orange nuggets of sugary, chewy sweets, and all nutritionally empty foods colored salmon, adobe, russet, or orange exude an aura that magnifies desirability. We women know how rouging our cheeks gives us an advantageous glow. Casting a warm rosy, adobe glow is appealing on foods as well as the face. Healthy food looks even more appealing under a candle's rosy luminescence.

Candlelight makes healthy food more appealing.

Suggested Cures

• Paint the ceiling over the dining table russet, adobe, or orange to reflect these colors onto the tabletop.

• Use an adobe tablecloth or place mats.

• Hang a picture with these tones across from your seat.

• Use candlelight instead of electric light at night.

• Purchase plates with these tones.

33. What sounds cause us to chew food slowly?

Low, deep sounds with regular but slow beats

Have you ever tried to quiet a group of chattering children? If you have, you probably screamed at the top of your lungs with a piercing sound that could be heard at the North Pole. I used to do the same—until I learned a more effective approach. Pounding a tabletop lightly with a slow, steady beat or uttering a low, consistent droning of a single word commands the same kind of attention and reduces frenzy as well. As drumbeats underscore music, voices tend to adopt the rhythm of repetitive sounds. Without even realizing it, we pace ourselves to match the cadence of the sounds around us.

In the same way the sound of a grandfather clock's pendulum swing, slow droplets of water onto a hard surface, or a metronome at its lowest tempo signals us to adopt a rhythmic pulse that slows us down. When mealtimes are accompanied by a languorous and repetitive beat, the pace of chewing will slow, and hence you are likely to eat less.

Suggested Cures

To help you slow down your chewing, install one of these items in your dining area:

- A clock that ticks

- A water fountain that drops water slowly onto a hard surface

- A wind chime pulsed by a slow fan

- A metronome

- Two strings with Ping-Pong balls or other hard objects attached to a slowly rotating fan

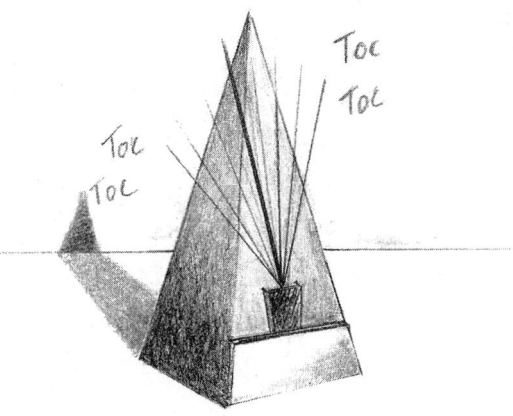

A metronome set to a slow beat will set a pace that encourages slower chewing and hence less food consumption.

34. What kind of artwork can reduce overeating?

A still life without food, a quiet winter scene, or any picture that radiates stillness

A tranquil ambience makes the dining experience a leisurely interlude.

Consider the view from your favorite dining room seat. What do you see? If it is a painting full of action and movement, you are actually being encouraged to chew faster and eat more, whereas a still life or a winter scene will reduce the desire to overeat.

You might be wondering why a winter scene works as well as a still life. In winter, the body slows down, hibernates if you will. Similarly, a winter motif exudes a message of calm, slow stillness. In feng shui tranquillity is considered a yin state that generates a calm, measured way of experiencing the world. Therefore scenes of mountains covered with white snow or trees laden with ice are yin and will discourage you from eating too quickly.

A tranquil still life that doesn't depict food in a dining room helps with weight maintenance.

Suggested Cures

• Hang a still life of flowers, a serene winter landscape, or a tranquil water scene without boats and their implied movement.

• Should your taste not run to any of these choices, consider hanging predominantly blue artwork (see Question 30). Select a picture with curved, undulating shapes, because these lines underscore tranquillity. Avoid geometric or straight lines, which tend to agitate.

35. What scent reduces hunger?

Mint

Most restaurants have mints available for their guests after dinner. Mint has the capacity to reduce our taste for other flavors, obliterating the craving for more. Have you ever eaten a peppermint together with another food? When I tried eating one with an egg, I found that I no longer wanted to finish the egg. Mint is an appetite suppressant.

Often we continue eating after we are full because the tastes linger, triggering a desire for more. If we could negate experiencing the taste, we could experience feeling satiated and thus stopping would not be as difficult.

Almost as potent as a peppermint candy, the smell of mint can curb overeating. Therefore carrying peppermint essential oil to inhale or burning mint essential oil can aid in dieting.

Suggested Cures

• Purchase mint essential oils and add several drops to a squirt bottle of water. Spray on any upholstery fabric in your dining area or on a cloth or paper napkin.

• Drink mint herbal tea if the munchies strike between meals.

• Consider using a mint hand cream so that you need to do nothing more than lift your hand to inhale its scent.

Mint is effective in stopping hunger and can be infused in oil and rolled under the nose to curb hunger.

• Use an aerating dispenser and spray the dining area just before the main course is served.

• There is a product called "I Feel Full" that can be carried in a handbag or briefcase that dispenses mint scent on a roller and can be rolled under the nose for an ongoing intense mint scent. See the Resources in the back of this book.

36. What types of views keep you aware of what and how much you are eating?

Yin rather than yang scenes

How many times have you looked down astonished at an empty plate of food after a lively bout of conversation? When we are absorbed in interesting and amusing conversation around the dinner table, some of us become so distracted that we pay no attention to how much food is consumed, and we tend to overeat. Of course, the solution is not to eat in complete silence but to face the most nonstimulating view possible.

What to face and what to avoid facing when dining can promote awareness of our eating pattern, enabling us to slow down and eat less.

Suggested Cures

- Position yourself to face a solid empty wall or an opening to another room or window, so long as the scene is serene.

- Try to be surrounded by blue, purple, and/or yellow.

- Don't face a busy street scene while eating.

- Avoid viewing a wall with more than three pictures or wall hangings.

- Stay visually away from the color red, orange, or green.

A seat with a long view can create the tranquillity necessary for
measured food consumption.

37. What patterns urge you to move or exercise?

Stripes

I will never forget a doctor's reply when I complained about my middle-age weight gain. Staring at me, he asked me to consider the difference between my body's movement level at that moment and the way a child might be acting while seated in the same chair. He pointed out that young people are usually in motion, typically wriggling, pumping their legs, and squirming in their seats, while I in midlife sat in complete stillness. Children aren't typically sedentary and expend more calories through activity than adults do.

While you can't turn back the clock, you can change an environment so that it inspires movement, helping you to burn up unwelcome calories. Stripes, particularly vertical or diagonal ones, inspire movement. No, not all walls in your home have to be covered with striped wallpaper. Rather, place objects with stripes in places where you typically sit.

The diagonal design of lattice inspires movement.

Suggested Cures

• While stripes in the dining area will increase the pace of eating, in areas where you want to exercise or act, stripes can inspire you to move.

• Place a striped vase atop a TV.

• Use lattice (which is really two rows of diagonal stripes) as a room divider within view of an easy chair.

• Line up small row of books across from your desk.

• Drink water from striped glasses.

38. What patterns make you eat faster?

Circles and dots

If you tend to shovel food down without a great deal of awareness, stay away from patterns with circles or dots. Observing a round object transfixes us more than any other shape. This is partly due to the fact that our survival instinct demands that we calculate how fast an object is moving. It takes keener observation to determine if a circular shape such as a stone is in motion than it does to realize that we are confronted with a loping tiger. Dots and circles, especially when repeated in a pattern, exaggerate this phenomenon because there is so much material to comprehend. A pattern that commands such concentrated attention can easily distract us from what we're doing, such as eating. The round shape in any form, in fact, whether it's glasses, plates, bowls, or vases, encourages us to think and express our thoughts, and we may become so involved in the subject matter that we ignore how much we eat.

Suggested Cures

• There are typically a great many objects with circles and dots present in many homes, but we are often unaware of their presence. Alter them especially if they exist in the dining area or any place you frequently eat.

- Change round knobs on cabinets to square in the dining room.

- Avoid round drinking glasses.

- Purchase square plates.

- Remove round bowls holding floral arrangements or round accessories in the center of the table.

- Use a boldly contrasting checkered tablecloth or mat.

- Select an undulating or square centerpiece.

- Use place mats in a color that matches the dishes, camouflaging the round shape. Because the color is extended, your eye will see only the overall shape.

Changing round knobs to square ones on dining or kitchen cabinets is an effective way of avoiding dots or circles, patterns that generate a fast eating pace.

39. Why should a kitchen not be seen from the entrance to a home?

Because viewing the kitchen will make the occupants more likely to overindulge

Food and love are closely associated. Even now, as an adult, one of the first things I do upon returning to my parents' home is to check to see what's in the refrigerator. In the same way, seeing a kitchen from the entrance to a home focuses attention on food.

Suggested Cures

If your kitchen can be seen from your home's entrance, moving the kitchen to another location is probably out of the question. Here are some alternatives:

- Build a false wall between the entrance and the kitchen.

- Place a screen in front of the kitchen's entrance.

- Make the kitchen door close automatically by installing a spring closing hinge.

- Light a painting intensely to draw the eye away from the direction of the kitchen.

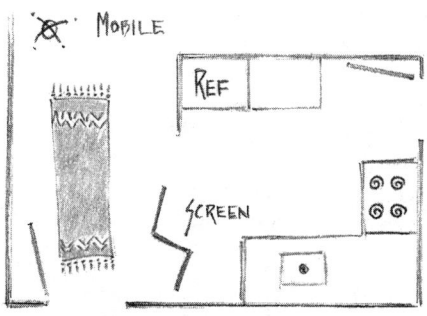

Be sure to direct the eye away from a kitchen at a home's entrance by either providing a distraction in the distance or screening the kitchen's interior.

• Place a coat rack, an answering machine, or any other interactive equipment just beyond the kitchen's entrance to give those who enter an alternative choice of action.

• Lay a runner from the entrance to a location past the kitchen.

• If your home has an alarm system, mount the control panel beyond the kitchen threshold so that you don't have to stop in a place where you can see the kitchen to turn off the alarm on your way in.

40. What helps you cut down on snacking while working at the kitchen sink?

A distant view, either to the outside or via a picture with a distant vanishing point

We spend a great deal of time working at or near a kitchen sink. Normally the focus is on food preparation. The desire to nosh while preparing the meal can be intensified by the proximity of the food. We have all excused little tastes of this and that, forgetting that tasting adds calories that usually go uncounted, preferring to believe that tiny nibbles don't count.

Therefore, it is helpful to have a distraction from food even though our attention is appropriately focused on preparation. A view with depth, movement, and the delights of nature is just what the feng shui practitioner would order.

Suggested Cures

If you have a window over the sink, you are all set. Otherwise, here are some other remedies:

• Hang a painting with a vanishing point, like a pathway leading to a distant mountain.

• Hang a landscape or a picture that replicates a natural setting. It will redirect the mind from food preparation to its positive image.

• Hang a small, bright, flat, shiny disk at eye level.

6

Ways to Overcome the Emotional Trauma of Death and Divorce

We cannot pass through life unscathed. We need lifelines to help us out of the mire of the difficult times created by loss. Loss impels us to dissolve the existing patterns in our lives, and in the physical environment, and replace them with ones that promote healing and appropriate change. Feng shui cures can offer assistance during these life passages.

41. What shape helps you feel less vulnerable after a loss?

Square

Loss and bereavement can literally sweep away your sense of support, leaving you with vulnerability that can be crippling. To counterbalance this debilitating sense of loss, it is imperative to introduce household furnishings and accessories that make you feel supported and grounded.

The square generates feelings of stability more than any other shape. With all sides the same length, it can withstand pressure applied at any point equally. Thus looking at a square can reground you.

Following a life crisis, it is best to find ways to promote stability and help yourself feel protected. Consider moving as many low, chunky, square objects as possible to where you will see them often. While grieving benefits the recovery process of healing, feeling stable will make its devastation easier.

Suggested Cures

• Cut rectangular place mats into squares.

• Place a square area rug under a cocktail table or on the floor near the side of the bed you use.

Chunky, square, low furniture and square area rugs and accessories provide a
sense of security that can be temporarily missing after a loss.

• Hang a square picture across from a frequently used chair.

• Should your dining chair have small railing-type arms, cover the opening with fabric to give the chair a solid look.

• Reposition your gathering room furnishings to make the overall shape a square.

42. What color should be removed from your home after loss of a spouse?

Orange

Marriage conceptually merges two people into a unit. Even though you have retained a personal identity in many life areas, there is a covert contract that the partnership is in many ways a single unit. Since orange is the color of fusion, it is best removed during the intense months following death or divorce.

Replace orange with blue for at least the first ninety days and you will be augmenting your personal self-worth and coping abilities.

Suggested Cures

• Cover orange-upholstered furniture with a blue throw, afghan, or piece of fabric.

• Exchange any pictures dominated by orange for ones using mainly blue.

• Add a variety of objects to your sight lines in different rooms that will support what you need. Be aware that most colors, including blue, are mixed with other color tones. Thus, by determining what tones are used you can fine-tune the message blue imparts:

Blue with yellow produces a sense of optimism.
Blue with red produces a sense of importance.
Blue with green produces a sense of being able to change.
Light blue connects the self to spirituality.
Dark blue encourages you to care for your health.

43. What color should you avoid reflecting in the light near mirrors after a loss?

Yellow

Seeing the color yellow or gold can produce optimism, but unless your skin tone is red, yellow cast on your reflection will give you a drained, unhealthy look. When suffering the effects of loss, we tend to feel less than positive about many things, ourselves included. Unfortunately, it is just at these times that change is often demanded of us. Like wearing apparel that sparks self-confidence, experiencing ourselves in the best light can rekindle the flame of optimism. Humans have a built-in survival tool of optimism no matter how deeply buried it may appear to be.

Suggested Cures

• Cover a lamp with a nonflammable paper or fabric near your dressing area's mirror, using the color that is best for you:

For dark skin (black or shades of brown without yellow), use red.
For olive skin with yellow overtones, use pink.
For pale white skin with overtones of red, use green.
For pale white skin without red overtones, use pink.

• Surround your mirror with the color appropriate to your skin tone either with paint or with fabric.

• Add an appropriately colored bulb in the light near mirrors.

44. What household chore should be done within a reasonable time after a loss?

Give away or throw away the other person's possessions

A great deal has been written about clutter and its negative implications. In general, clutter hinders change because it represents holding on, symbolizes the fear of letting go, hampers the development of tools for change, and prevents you from moving on.

While honoring the positive from that which is no longer in your life—and all experiences have a nugget of value—it is important to remove anything that keeps you chained to the past. After a loved one's death, emptying his or her closet, dresser, and desk will be a cathartic experience, as it will also after a divorce.

You don't have to move on this the day or even the week after the loss, but it is best to complete all sorting and discarding within eighteen months after a significant person is no longer with you.

Suggested Cures

After the death of a loved one

• Keep only a few favored items such as a paperweight, perfume, letters, or articles of clothing.

Establishing a "new" life is difficult unless the material possessions of the person no longer there have been removed.

• Donate anything useful to nonprofit thrift shops, historical libraries, or homeless shelters.

• Give things away to those who knew the person. Everyone connected with that person might be thrilled to receive one memento from his or her life.

After a divorce

• Give your former spouse a reasonable date by which he or she should remove all personal items. If that date is not met, do it yourself.

• Let your children take what they want and toss the rest out or donate it.

• Box up anything of material or sentimental value and ship it out to your ex-spouse's new location.

45. How many chairs should there be at a dining table after a loss?

No more than enough chairs for the people or person who will be dining there daily plus two extra

If eating were just a matter of staying alive, we probably would take no more notice of it than we do our breathing. However, it is more often an occasion for contact and interaction with others. In many cases breakfast and lunch are occasions to be with family, friends, or colleagues, and dinner is sometimes the only time families spend together.

Since I travel a great deal, I eat many meals by myself. Eating dinner alone often evokes sympathetic nods from other diners. Counters and bars help dissipate the feeling of isolation because one faces a server rather than an empty chair.

When we are newly bereaved, the missing person's presence is often felt more keenly at mealtimes. When there are more than two extra chairs, the void magnifies the loss.

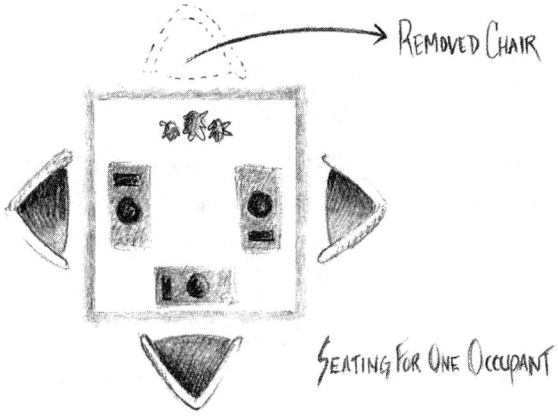

REMOVED CHAIR

SEATING FOR ONE OCCUPANT

To avoid feeling lonely, have no more than two extra chairs at the dining table.

Suggested Cures

• Occupy the chair formerly used by the other.

• Reposition extra chairs elsewhere, either against a wall, next to another piece of furniture like a breakfront or serving counter, or in another room.

• Face action and avoid a static scene—this is one of those times when watching television can be beneficial, but a window or an action-oriented piece of artwork can also help.

46. What changes should be made in a bedroom following a loss?

As many as possible as quickly as possible after a divorce; more gradual change after a death

If the person shared the bedroom with you, it is imperative to alter this room. Implied in the space are the patterns of movements, thoughts, and interactions that had been, and these will block you from altering the present appropriately.

Suggested Cures

• Move the bed to another wall so long as the movement doesn't place the bed in a bad feng shui position. In general, a bed should be positioned so its occupant can see the entrance door to the room easily. If that is not possible, hang a mirror or reflective object to allow you to see the entrance in its reflection when in bed.

• Purchase new sheets and throw away, donate, or use the old ones as rags.

• At the very least, reverse the mattress and if possible purchase a new mattress and headboard within nine months.

• Remove all of the other's person's things from the nightstand and move some of your personal items there immediately.

• Empty the dresser and closet and, if you can't let the contents go, store them in cartons elsewhere.

• Reposition some artwork.

• Draw back window treatments during daylight hours.

• Position a wind chime so it moves in the breezes coming through a window or hang it near an air duct.

47. What should be added to every room after a loss?

An item that responds to air movement to break the stillness

Life begets life. When suffering the aftermath of a loss, infuse energy into a space in the same way nature does. In nature the most life-affirming places are those that afford a varied and profuse interaction. The desert has little but sand and the North Pole little but snow, but in temperate and tropical areas with fertile soil, sufficient water, and a growing season, leaves flutter, branches sway, songbirds trill, and grasses rustle in the wind. In short, movement is life affirming.

Stillness in many forms is the enemy of healing. Therefore, after a divorce or death it is important to surround yourself with as many sensual experiences as possible.

Suggested Cures

For movement

• Locate a plant in the rooms you use and direct a fan on it.

• If there are lightweight curtains, point a fan in their direction, especially if the windows are kept shut.

• Hang a mobile from the ceiling near a door so the air moves it when the door is opened or hang it from a window you typically keep cracked open.

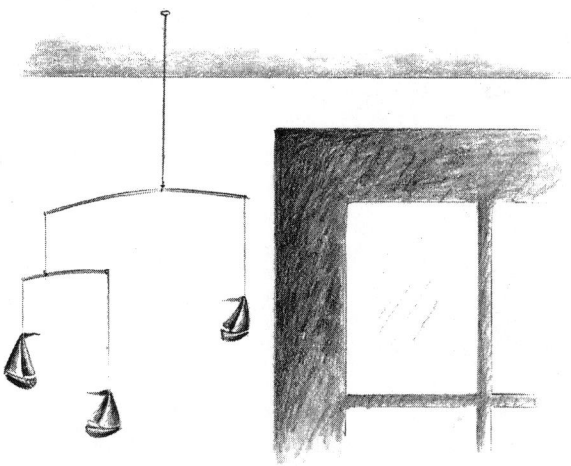

Having a lightweight mobile fills a home with a sense of life and is an antidote to the void experienced after loss of a family member.

- Purchase a recirculating fountain or make one from a small pump bought from a pet supply store and submerge it in a bowl of water.

For sound

- Turn the TV on to the weather channel. The announcers change every twenty minutes and replicate real voices more than entertainment channels.

- Acquire a pet bird—or any pet for that matter.

- Loop bells over the handles of the doors and cabinets used daily. Be sure they have different sounds so that each place has its distinct tone.

For scents

- Commercial products create scents replicating grass, mud, corn, or just about any organic substance. Use scents that replicate a natural habitat you love, such as

Pine for forests
Gardenia or rose for flower gardens
Grass for picnicking
Sea Breeze for the seaside

48. What changes should be made to the entrance of a home after a loss?

Remove any decoration hanging on or next to the door and replace with another that reflects other or different personal interests or aesthetics

The entrance to a home reflects the people who live inside. Often we get an impression of the residents of a home just from the art or accessories outside. We are subtly yet profoundly affected by the images we first see when entering a home.

Look carefully at the icons that are affixed to the walls, the choice of nameplate, doorbell, knocker, holiday decorations, as well as any furnishings and garden decor to determine how the missing person is represented and ascertain whether or not to retain this expression. Only when the icons are affirming or loved should they remain.

Suggested Cures

• Add a fixture or an icon in yellow, the color of optimism, such as a shiny brass ornament.

• Fix anything that is visibly broken.

• Repaint the front door a different color.

• Purchase a new doormat.

• Add at least three new ornaments of your choosing, such as a wreath, flag, or new mailbox, to the exterior entrance.

• Add a new garden ornament to the front lawn.

Change a minimum of three things at the exterior entrance after a divorce or death. Be certain that the icons reflect your interests.

49. How can you use light to help you heal after death or divorce?

Fill your home with both sunlight and electric light and drench the perimeter of your home with light at night

Consider how vital sunlight is to vegetation's growth. Consider how many skin ailments improve with sunlight and how some forms of depression are actually triggered by lack of light and can be remedied with light therapy. Letting sunlight into the home is one of the best defenses against feeling blue. In the Jewish religion, during the first seven days after a death in the family the survivors close all curtains and cover all mirrors. This makes sense, for in the first week after the loss it is appropriate to grieve and feel the pain. Suppressing these feelings is harmful, for what

Shining a light to dispel darkness can melt away the despair that is often experienced when the sun goes down.

is suppressed comes back to haunt us. We need to grieve after a death or divorce before the healing can begin. Thus cutting off your connection to normal life and not being able to see yourself in a mirror is appropriate right after the death of a loved one. After this intense period has passed, however, the opposite environmental experience is what is needed for us to move on.

Suggested Cures

• During the day, open curtains, pull up shades, and move obstructions that are blocking sunlight.

• Mount a spotlight outside the home to illuminate the exterior, bathing your outdoor surroundings in light during the nighttime.

• Hang yellow curtains so they will give the illusion of light when nighttime demands privacy.

50. What scents reduce feelings of confusion and haziness?

Eucalyptus, hyssop, myrrh, marjoram, pine

All scents are associated with one of feng shui's five elements. The metal element helps clarify mental processes and stimulates the gathering of information and the shaping of ideas. Choosing one of the metal element scents helps you focus on the solutions you may need following a loss and keeps you engaged in mitigating emotional pain.

Suggested Cures

• Stew eucalyptus leaves in a simmering pot of water to help you overcome the inability to move forward and to enhance your ability to relinquish whatever no longer serves you.

• Purchase hyssop essential oil and use it on a scent ring—the kind that rests on a lamp's lightbulb—to dispel gloom and negativity and improve concentration by invigorating your mind and reducing nervous exhaustion.

• Choose a toothpaste with the herb myrrh (found in health food stores), because it has a powerful effect on the nervous system and reaches into the psyche to help us transcend and transform aspects of material existence.

• Find a sachet containing marjoram and use it on a desk, under your pillow, or in another area where concentration is required. Marjoram can release tensions and quell worry when you're under pressure (that's why it traditionally has been used at weddings). This herb is effective in reducing insomnia and grief.

• Light pine candles to help you let go of what is old and useless and to restore confidence. Pine also helps reverse short-term memory loss. Finally, it restores a positive self-identity and promotes a vibrant self-image.

7

Ways to Convey a Positive Image to the Neighborhood

The image your home projects to neighbors affects how they treat you. Being treated affirmatively is central to overall contentment. When my new neighbors placed a large welcome sign at the base of their front steps and painted their front door a bright lime green, it signaled to the neighborhood that they were approachable and friendly. This couple quickly became an integral part of our neighborhood. Because your neighborhood is an extended personal environment, it is important to consider what your home's exterior communicates.

51. What feature promotes neighborhood camaraderie?

Sidewalks or footpaths between neighbors' homes

The essence of neighborhood is the concept of connectedness, or Tao. Simplistic as this may sound, none of us could survive happily without connections to our community. In fact not one iota of life as we know it would survive were it not for a network of connections. In the most profound way, failing to sustain connections means riding against the tide of life.

My childhood neighborhood left me with a lasting impression of the benefits of connectedness. Our street, Burnett Terrace, had formed an association whose sole function was social. I knew every family who lived

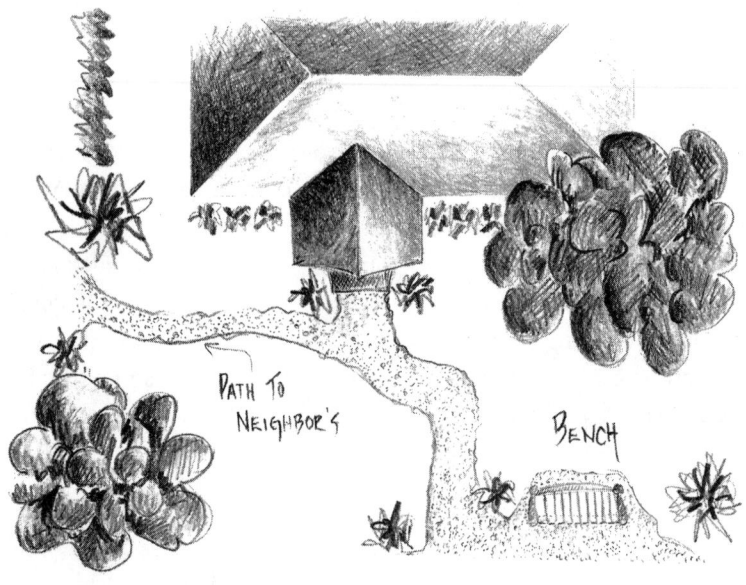

Thriving is supported by extended associations; thus, adding a pathway across your property to a neighbor or placing a bench in the front yard invites activity and supports connectedness.

on this half-mile length of road. Life was secure and embracing because I was known and knew my neighbors. My present neighborhood replicates this experience, and I am certain I purchased my home today because I realized that the tiny neighborhood in which it is located evoked my early positive experiences.

Suggested Cures

• If sidewalks don't exist in your neighborhood, consider making a portion of your front yard a walkway or an obvious meeting place. Clear away a portion of grass and replace it with gravel or some other paving material.

• Place an actual bench or a plank over two logs in your front yard, inviting people to occupy outdoor, front-of-the house space.

• Create mini-encounters such as a table holding a bountiful crop of tomatoes or extra flower bulbs removed after weeding out a daffodil bed, free for the taking.

52. How can fencing bolster a sense of self?

By articulating your boundaries

Many years ago, when I was searching for a new home, the realtor asked what my requirements were. My reply was simple. I wanted to feel as if I could walk out my front door naked and not be seen by neighbors. I meant that metaphorically, of course. I simply wanted to feel free and to communicate my nonnegotiable personal boundaries.

In the same way, finding a way to enclose your property or home is an aid to feeling free. My sister lives in an apartment, and her former neighbor one floor below had a fixation about footsteps. She discovered this proclivity when her renovation included stripping carpeting off the natural wood floors. In just a few days her neighbor started complaining that the footsteps were driving him crazy, and since the condominium supported this kind of complaint my sister literally had to tiptoe around her home. It was a most unpleasant time and added a great deal of stress to her life. Finally, she admitted defeat and reinstalled carpet on the floors.

Sight and sound privacy are essential to feeling free in your own home. While fences are normally thought of as property line markers, in feng shui we think of fences three-dimensionally. If you can't sing at the top of your lungs, walk from the bathroom to your bedroom naked, or watch TV until the sun comes up without disturbing a neighbor, then some kind of fence is needed. Think of a fence as protection from having to accommodate the needs of others more than your own.

Suggested Cures

- Fence the yard if possible.

- Install curtains that cover all or part of a window.

- Apply cork on a wall to deaden sounds between rooms or neighbors, as well as sheers that block details but let light in.

- Put up a trellis outside a window to screen the inside.

- If your apartment is over another's, consider using large area carpets over floors that are used frequently.

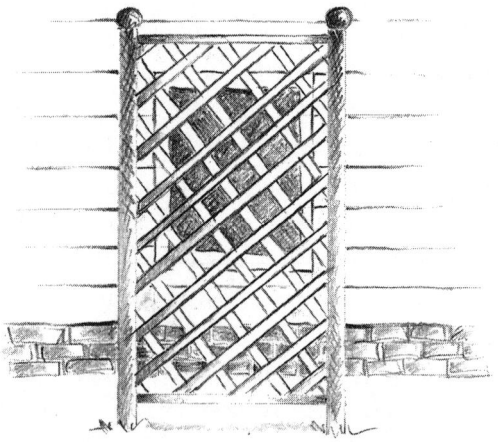

A trellis outside a window affords privacy but does not signal
unfriendliness as do continuously closed curtains.

- Position a folding screen inside a window that faces driving or walking areas outside.

53. What image does a fence communicate?

The nature of the family's emotional boundaries

Psychologists tell us that personal boundaries are critical in relationships. In a physical space with a public presence, fences can establish the nature of families' boundaries. The choice of fence conveys the way a person or family feels about intimacy and what values or choices the occupants are comfortable with in order to feel close. The choice of a fence's design and color communicates a message. Be sure to encircle your property with a fence whose message best supports what you fundamentally are.

Suggested Cures

- Use a picket fence to demonstrate that you are traditional yet flexible.

- Install a chain link to say that this family needs a great deal of privacy.

- Select a stockade-style fence if you are emotionally reserved.

- Choose stone or brick as a fencing material if you want others to know you as reliable and dependable.

- The choice of a split-rail fence divides but does not imply an unwillingness to be approached.

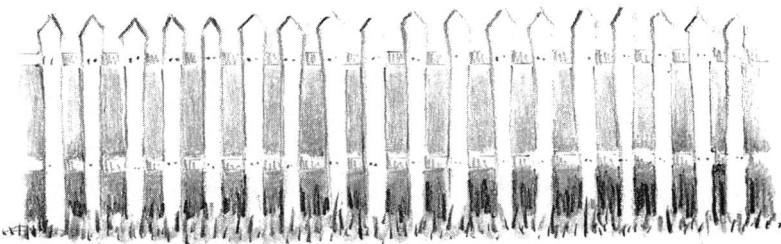

A picket fence communicates valuing tradition while still being open to change.

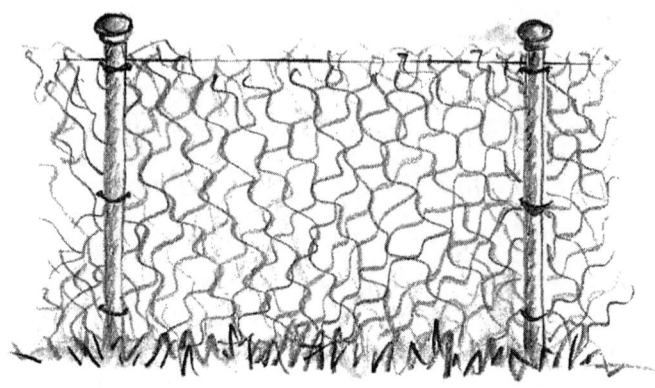

Chain-link fencing communicates a strong desire for privacy.

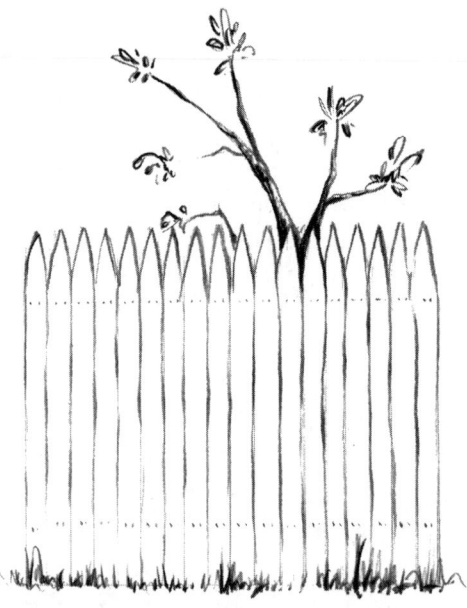

Stockade fencing signals that the residents are less willing to expose
their emotional selves to others.

Those who want to be known as reliable and dependable often choose stone or brick fencing.

A split-rail fence communicates a sense of personal territory without imposing a desire for emotional distance.

54. What does a straight pathway to the front door communicate?

That the occupants' lives are often stressful and they are not in as much control over their lives as they could be

Walking down a passage without bends or undulations leaves no room for surprises or distractions. When the shape of a path does nothing to reduce a walker's pace, the approach is likely to be hurried and less satisfying. People who retain or choose a straight path are likely to live hurried and busy lives. Less time implies less attention to focusing on self as well as others.

Reshaping a straight path with planters communicates a relaxed presence and the desire to be make others comfortable.

Further, if a pathway is long because a house is set back significantly from the street, then a straight path tends to aggrandize the occupants. Seeing a door at the end of a long road lengthens the anticipation and distances the traveler from the destination.

Suggested Cures

Should any of these implications not reflect your desires, here's how you can create an undulating path:

• Clear the area alongside the path in an undulating shape, then fill with materials in a color similar to that of the walkway. The path will appear reshaped.

• Place a planter, sundial, or any object that is sized appropriately to interrupt a direct progression down the path.

• Cover part of an existing straight walkway with a trellis or another overhead shelter to alter experience along the path.

55. What can you do if you require privacy but your exposures are extensive because you live in a house on a corner lot?

Obscure private windows and deflect attention elsewhere

While a corner lot usually has prominent neighborhood presence, it also has greater exposure. Providing privacy is the challenge if you are not comfortable with having attention directed at your residence.

Suggested Cures

To avoid feeling like you live in a fish bowl or that you have to hide behind curtains when windows face the street, you can employ these feng shui techniques for balancing exposure with privacy:

• Construct an upright lattice near windows, especially outside bedrooms, bathrooms, or other private spaces. This will allow light to penetrate but communicate the need for separateness.

• Consider a row of tall plants blocking out the scenes seen in windows.

• Distract the eye from the home to the edge of the property where the sidewalk or lawn meets the street by creating an undulating garden bed with either unusual plantings or garden art.

56. What home location is stressful unless you want the position of sentry for your neighborhood?

A home at a T-juncture or the first apartment next to the elevator or stairs

The vulnerability and exposure of the person in the middle of the circle during a game of dodge ball is not unlike being in a home at the end of a T-juncture or a road that if continued uninterrupted would wind up going through your house. Aside from the annoying presence of nighttime headlights aimed directly at the home, there is always a feeling of being unable to escape observation. A home situated at the T-juncture makes the occupants feel as if they are always in the public eye. This is precisely what it must feel like to be a well-known movie star in public.

Living in an apartment that forces you to take notice of other occupants coming and going can also place undue strain on you. A home is a refuge, and most of us demand that it fulfill some of our need for sanctuary. On the other hand, if you like being in charge or you like the limelight, you might find this location favorable. If not, and you lead the typical hectic, obligation-filled modern life, you'll want some downtime when at home.

Suggested Cures

Mitigate the effects of a T-juncture by:

- keeping the curtains closed on the lower half of the street-facing windows

- redirecting the pathway leading from the front door away from the T-juncture

- planting a hedge or a tree with low-growing limbs to block the road

- positioning a birdhouse outside the window facing the street

- arranging frequently used seating so that it doesn't face the street

To muffle the sounds of apartment neighbors' comings and goings:

- use a sound buffer like a water feature in an apartment to override the sounds of the elevator and footsteps

- hang a wind chime inside the front window and direct a fan to keep it moving

If a roadway is directly in front of your front door, reposition a path so that when either coming or going you will not be directly in front of the T-juncture. Leaving your home directly facing a street can make you feel defensive, and when returning home the same T-juncture is likely to make you feel unprotected.

57. What features of a facade signal unfriendliness and inaccessibility?

Absence of front windows or front windows that are always covered

Who hasn't peered into a street-facing window? Looking into a home's front windows is in some ways the same as peering into another person's eyes. Both reveal the inner self. A home designed with no windows facing the street denies others a connection to the inhabitants' souls.

With appropriate restraints, some street-facing windows should be undraped some of the time to communicate accessibility and a desire to be connected with your neighbors. There are ways to re-create a sense of connection without obliterating all privacy.

Suggested Cures

• Hang easily identifiable items that express who you are, such as a holiday decoration, a team's banner, or unique artwork.

• Place in clear view items obviously meant to be used by a visitor, such as an umbrella stand or a hanging basket with notepad and pencil for leaving messages.

If friendliness is a desired communication, have articles by your front door that are obviously meant for others' convenience.

58. What does a double or very tall entrance door communicate?

A desire to be viewed as socially superior

Large, high front doors seem to be increasingly popular in new home construction. Such doors may be a seductive selling tool, for they associate the home with major edifices such as churches, castles, and universities. Tall or double doors reflect the number of people who pass through them. Public buildings are appropriately fitted with grand entrances, while in a home an oversized entrance door can be intimidating for those who live there as well as those who visit. Implied is that the occupants' status will match the importance of the entrance. Visitors may sense that those living there are unapproachable. Whether these are the signals you want to send is up to you. Some people, residents and visitors alike, would welcome an elevation in status and be empowered by passing through an imposing doorway.

Suggested Cures

To make a door appear smaller

- use a contrasting color for the door trim

- paint the upper third a darker color than the lower portion, so long as there is appropriate trim or detail that can be used as the separating line

- paint an oval in a contrasting color on the door five or six feet from the ground

To make a door appear larger

- hang vertical decorations on it slightly higher than head level

- paint a faux transom above the door

- hang a wreath or some other decoration above the doorjamb

59. What shape home is a deterrent to personal change?

A U-shaped home or one with all rooms facing an interior courtyard

U-shaped homes or ones with all windows and major doors exiting into an interior setting are likely to encourage the status quo because the view is internal rather than other directed. Consider where these types of buildings predominate: China, Spain, the Middle East, South America, and Bali—all cultures that typically preserve the status quo and support traditional values. In our Western culture, which generally supports more iconoclastic behavior, homes usually front the street.

People who want to change and disengage from the past should live in a home without an inner courtyard.

Suggested Cures

If your house is a U-shaped home or one with a courtyard and it would be advantageous for you to change, here's what you can do:

- Plant vegetation to obscure the view across the courtyard.

- Reposition the interior seating away from courtyard window.

- Install a flag or other wind-responsive cloth in the courtyard.

If change is a desired goal and your home is U-shaped, install a flag on a pole in the interior courtyard to stimulate and inspire the desired transformation.

60. What do second-story bedrooms protruding over the first floor convey?

A sense of inequality and disunity

The amount of space allotted to various rooms in a house signals the value we place on those parts of the home. Visually, we are also drawn to any architectural oddity or to the proportionately largest part of a structure. Thus, upstairs bedrooms hanging over the lower floor signal the importance of the rooms upstairs over those downstairs.

Suggested Cures

Should your home have an overhanging second floor, here's what you can do to communicate unity and equality:

- Install imposing light fixtures outside, under the line of the overhang.

- Plant dramatic vegetation on the pathway to the downstairs entrance at the juncture of the overhang.

- Paint the lower level's window trim and door a highly contrasting lighter color than the upper level.

- Widen the path to the front door.

- Keep the window treatments closed on the second floor and allow a view inside through the windows on the first floor.

To communicate that the group is more important than the individuals, install significant electric lights or two large plants at the ground level of a home with the second floor overhanging the first.

61. What type of plantings directly in front of a home's entrance door is damaging to self-esteem?

A tree in line with and within a few steps of the front door

So many feng shui books scare the living daylights out of people by talking about bad chi. As discussed in Chapter 1, chi describes how we experience the environment. Since we absorb our surroundings through our senses, it stands to reason that when our sensorial system is limited or inadequate we feel less alive, and often this prevents us from reaching our maximum potential. Consider how you feel outside as compared to inside. The full sensorial input experienced outside feels so much more satisfying than the limited amount received inside. The sun's warmth,

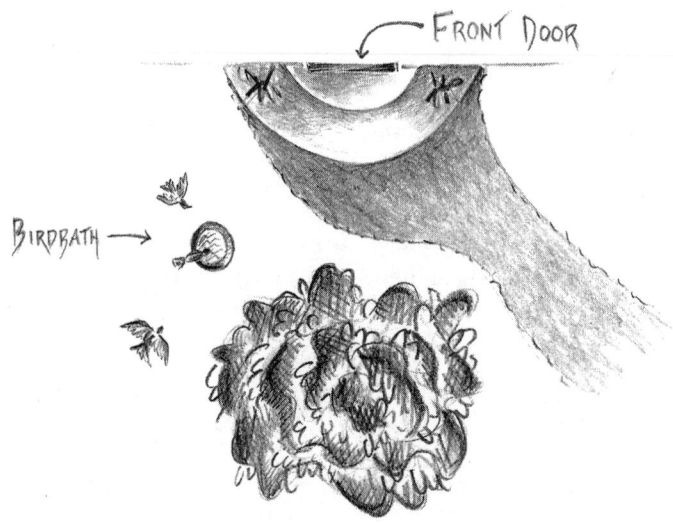

Any large object blocking sight and encumbering free movement from a home's entrance undermines your belief in your ability to overcome obstacles. By positioning a birdbath or anything that attracts the eye elsewhere, you lessen the effect of the blockage.

the intermittent sounds of birds and animals, and the scents and sights of plants add to the pleasure of being alive.

If a tree blocks full visual access when leaving home or your movement is restricted in any way, you will feel diminished and may consequently start to feel inadequate.

Suggested Cures

• Redirect the path to the door by turning it to face away from the tree.

• Hang a door chime on the tree to compensate and lessen focus on the blockage.

• Position a birdbath or hang a wind sock on either side of the tree to draw the eye away from the tree. The eye seeks out movement before a stationary object.

8

How Doors, Stairs, and Windows Influence Emotional States

Windows, doors, and stairways are features of transition. We look out windows, pass through doors, and travel to another level on staircases. Change generates increased emotional investment because it requires us to alter, adjust, or begin. Shifting gears requires more energy than remaining the same. When we are required to change, there is an increased likelihood that our vulnerabilities will surface or that we will not have the stamina to alter behavior appropriately. For these reasons, it is important to ascertain if the doors, windows, and staircases in your home have challenging elements to contend with. Self-assurance, a feeling of safety, family unity and contentment, and even digestive problems can be affected by imbalances in these areas.

62. Why do doors facing each other but slightly off center diminish confidence?

Because being askew produces a feeling of instability, which undermines self-confidence

Try staring at an object by covering one eye and then the other and notice how the image seems to jump positions depending on which eye is observing it. The misalignment created when entering through one door or threshold and seeing another exit slightly askew from the one entered is not unlike viewing an object with one eye and then the other. One is likely to feel less grounded and secure and hence less confident.

A fixed physical environment untroubled by visual uncertainties is necessary to support a secure sense of self. Subtle imbalances disturb the sense of equilibrium and render us less assured.

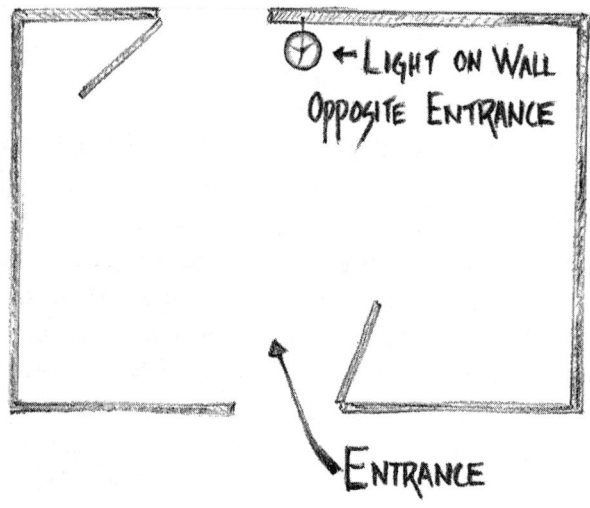

Balance an unbalanced view of two doors not directly across from each other by positioning a light on the same side as the door you enter.

Suggested Cures

- Hang a tall painting directly across from the door entered most frequently.

- Position a tall plant in the bull's-eye center of the visual path from one door to the other.

- Mount a light directly across from the door entered. This light will create balance by drawing the eye to the spot where the other door would be if it were in line with the one entered.

- Hang a row of pictures on the side of the door facing the one entered.

63. How far should a door open to produce a feeling of personal safety?

Flat against an adjacent wall

Everything we see and experience is filtered through the question "Am I safe?" If you have ever been startled by a strange sound, pulled your hand away after touching an unfamiliar texture, or involuntarily recoiled from an unusual smell, then you have experienced a spontaneous reaction.

An open door that does not fold back completely against an adjoining wall, especially at the entrance to a home, is detrimental to a feeling of safety. The automatic nervous system becomes aroused when there is even a hint of trouble, and panic reactions are triggered. Over time a home with such doors exerts subtle additional stress on its occupants.

Suggested Cures

Here are some ways to compensate if you cannot rehang a door to allow it to swing flat against an adjacent wall:

- Mount a large spring from the door to the wall and hang bells from it. It will subconsciously reassure you there is no danger lurking behind it.

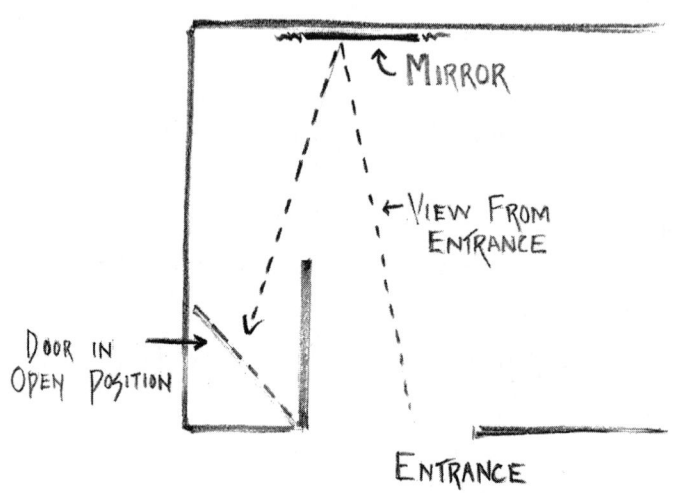

If a door cannot be fully opened, mount a mirror to reflect what is behind it and mitigate the subconscious unease that unseen space engenders.

- Hang wind chimes in the open space behind the door.

- Rehang the door to open to the other side should that side permit it to open fully.

- Affix a mirror across from the entrance to reveal the space behind the door.

64. What kind of bathroom lock promotes the greatest feelings of security?

A visible bolt rather than an interior lock

If I had my way, every single stall in every public rest room in the world would have a slide bolt on the interior of the doors instead of a concealed lock that secures the door. Many of us are uneasy when we are alone in a public bathroom and while using the toilet cannot reach the door. We often wonder if the door will stay shut. A visible, operative latch on a bathroom door quells these misgivings and may even prevent digestive problems from worsening owing to fears about compromised security.

Suggested Cures

• Install a slide bolt on all doors you typically lock, especially bathroom doors.

• Place a screen between the bathroom door and the toilet to obscure the view.

• Loop a bell on the outside door latch to produce a sound should someone outside use it.

• Hang a plant from the ceiling between the toilet and door.

• Lower the light wattage over the toilet and increase it in the location farthest from it.

• Hang a curtain to separate the toilet from the door.

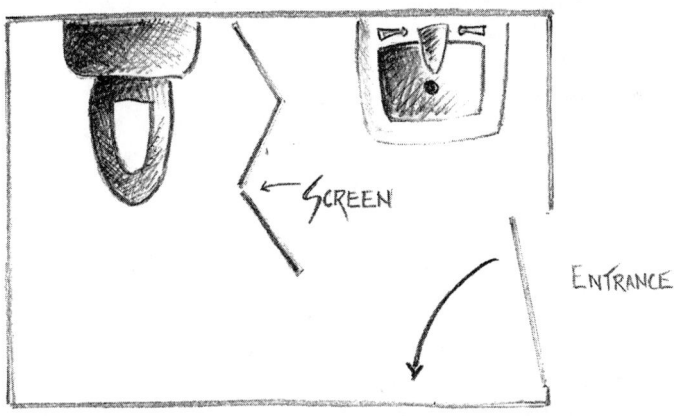

Screen the toilet from the entrance to a bathroom and mitigate any discomfort being exposed might generate.

65. When does the direction in which a door opens communicate unfriendliness?

When the door swings open toward those entering the space

Florida law requires a front door to swing outward instead of inward. The reasoning is that in a hurricane the hinges are less likely to give way under the wind's stress if they are on the outside of the door frame. That consideration aside, doors should open inward into a room. In other words, it should be more inviting to enter than exit.

A door that swings outward toward you requires you to move out of the way as it opens and forces you to step back before stepping forward. This action triggers a feeling of being on guard. To be pushed away before entering does nothing to emphasize welcome.

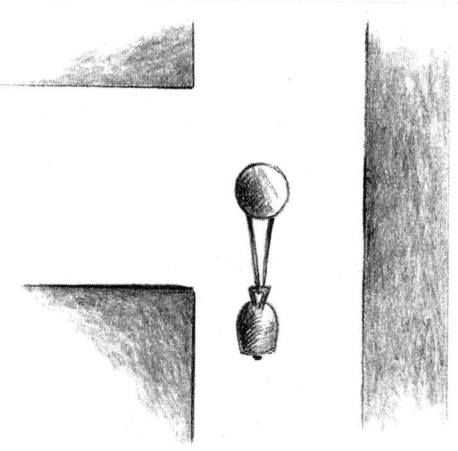

A bell adds a sensorial signal to a door that swings out toward the person entering, distracting you from being annoyed when you have to step back before coming in.

Suggested Cures

It is usually not very difficult to reverse the swing by rehanging a door, but if you can't do it, here are some alternatives:

- Place an area rug about two footsteps from the threshold.

- Lower the wattage in a lamp near the door or in an overhead light.

- Loop a bell over the handle of the door to distract attention from the less-than-favorable door swing.

66. When can the position of a staircase disrupt family unity?

When the staircase is seen as soon as you enter your home

A home is an intimate community, and when there are several members the community is knitted via the shared spaces. The gathering space is the epicenter of the family community, and when entering the home all paths should lead to it, not to alternate areas. In traditional two-story houses staircases typically lead to private spaces. If you proceed up the stairs, you will be disconnected from community spaces.

Suggested Cures

If you can see a staircase upon entering your home, there are a few ways to counteract the effect and enhance family cohesiveness:

- Hang a shiny or light-refracted object from the ceiling beyond the staircase and in the direction of the main gathering space.

- Lower the light wattage over the staircase and install a motion detector that will turn the light on only when someone uses the staircase.

- Place a runner over the floor area leading away from the staircase, such as down a hall to the gathering room.

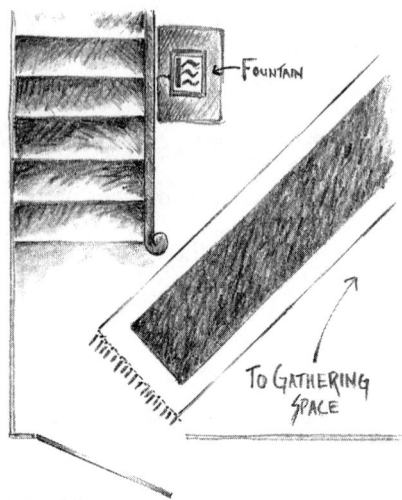

To enhance a family's cohesiveness, divert attention from a staircase positioned near a home's entrance and emphasize the path to the gathering space.

• Place a recirculating fountain just past the staircase toward a gathering space.

• Dispense vanilla or spiced apple scent or other familiar and loved scents in the gathering room.

67. What feature of staircases makes people feel burdened?

Stairs with high risers (seven or more inches), making the climb up arduous and the climb down unstable

When I traveled to Asia, I was startled by the height of steps on most Buddhist temple stairs. Since Asians tend to be smaller in stature than Westerners, I was puzzled as to why the risers were higher than ours. Finally one day a lightbulb was turned on, and I realized that higher-than-normal treads make a climb slower and so promote more aware-ness. It is an arduous process to achieve spiritual awareness, and the dif-ficult climb parallels this journey.

Suggested Cures

Should you have a staircase with high risers and not want to incur the expense of tearing it down and rebuilding another, here are some suggestions:

• Display things that entertain, entice, or just plain amuse to divert people's attention from the physical annoyance of a difficult climb.

• Mount a grouping of engaging photos on the wall adjacent to or atop the landing.

• Hang an object that moves, such as a mobile, clocks, or a wind chime, above the stairs.

Compelling photos or artwork can make climbing a steep staircase feel easier.

• Mount highly contrasting or brightly colored artwork with words or messages on a distant wall. Just like seeing large newspaper headlines, we naturally focus on something to read, transforming the climb into a secondary experience.

68. What kind of staircase causes confusion and doubt?

A spiral staircase

Twirl around three times in place and most likely you will feel dizzy. Spiral staircases spin you around as you proceed up or down. While the speed doesn't necessarily match that of twirling in place, it is an unstable way to proceed. In a home with a spiral staircase, especially one without solid risers, the subliminal message that is reinforced is of

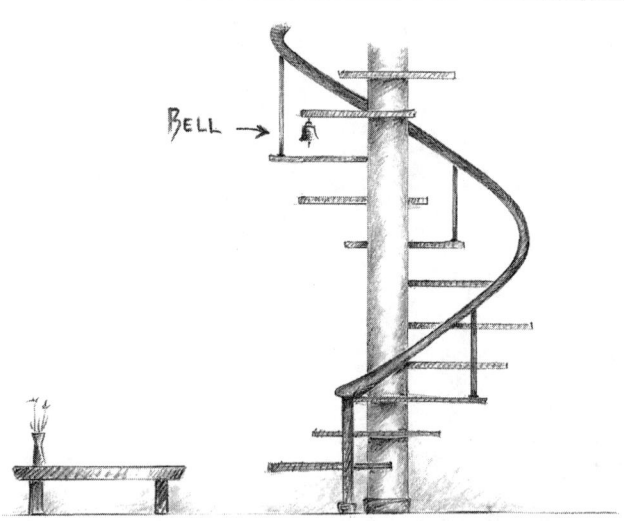

Spiral stairs are stressful, but you can make them less so by using sound devices that will be engaged when you mount the steps.

confusion and hence doubt, which may seep into your concerns about other life issues. Feng shui works because the patterns we establish in a physical environment reinforce the ones we cling to emotionally. Thus, even without a tendency to be doubtful and puzzled, a physical pattern that creates dizziness has the potential to be detrimental on an emotional level.

Suggested Cures

Tearing down and rebuilding a staircase is wildly expensive and may very well be impractical since spiral stairs are usually chosen to begin with when there is insufficient space for other stairs. There are, however, things you can do to improve the experience:

• Duplicate on all levels frequently used items such as scissors, tape, string, pens and paper, flashlight, candles, phone books, and bottled drinks (water, soda, etc.). In other words, do whatever it takes to reduce the number of necessary trips between floors.

• Mount a sound-producing device like a bell under the midpoint of the stairs. A repeated sound becomes a gauge announcing the distance covered, which focuses attention on what is accomplished.

• Weighty, low objects at the two termination points, such as a statue, a planter with draping vines, or a deeply colored small area rug, underscore stability and lessen the pattern of confusion created.

69. What window placement tends to increase the likelihood of others ignoring or disregarding your opinions?

Windows behind you when you sit

When seated against an active window scene you will likely be ignored or disregarded because those facing you will be drawn to the distant light and movement outside.

Place an enticing object in front of seating that is backed by a window.

While adults have more control over their attention than children, kids are easily distracted by everything from a squirrel scurrying up a tree trunk to a traffic light changing colors. When a window frames you, keeping others' attention, even adults', is difficult.

Suggested Cures

• Close the curtains if doing so would not make the room gloomy, or reposition the seats facing away from the window if practical.

• Mount a ticking clock on a wall away from the window to provide a predictable repetitive sound to ground those who might be distracted by the window.

• Hang a mobile under an air duct or position a fan on it away from the windows but within the sight line of those facing the seat against the window.

• Place floating candles or flowers (or toy ducks for that matter) in a bowl on a table in front of the seat with its back to the window.

70. What furniture/window configuration used in the afternoon prevents optimal completion of tasks?

Seating at a table that faces west

During my childhood our family physician advised my mother to take a sick child's temperature at 4:00 P.M. to determine when a bout of illness had abated. If our temperature was normal, we were pronounced well. Even without an illness, humans generally experience more physical and emotional stress in the late afternoon than at other times of day. Therefore, if you are required to perform a task during that time period, be it homework, dinner preparation, practice, or work, there are some feng shui keys to sustaining optimal performance.

Suggested Cures

The most important cure is to position yourself away from the direct glare of the setting sun. Be it the heat or the glare, a setting sun shining in your eyes only adds to the stress of these hours. If you cannot do that, try these suggestions:

- Block the sun's rays with a window treatment that can be pulled up from the bottom.

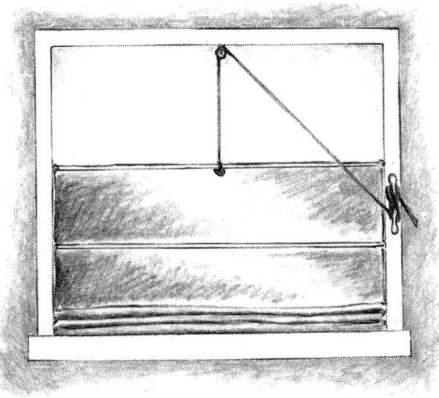

If you sit near a west-facing window, especially in the afternoon, install a window covering that can be pulled from the bottom up to protect yourself from the stress of facing the setting sun.

- Take two standard picture frames and tack an opaque cloth where a picture would be mounted, then hinge them together to make a work surface screen to block the sun's rays.

- Fill a tall ceramic, stone, or metal vase and place a fan-shaped plant in it to act as a sunscreen.

71. Why are more than three windows in a dining room detrimental?

Because windows are distractions and the family members will either disregard those seated in front of them or be distracted from conversation

The dining table is the last bastion for family conversation for most of us. Anything that potentially distracts is a detriment to what is so necessary for sustaining a bond. While we contemporary Westerners love to have lots of glass, we are also setting up a pattern of focusing outside family life. Isn't it true that most of us spend far more time engaged in activities outside the home than with our families? Thus the reduction of windows in a dining area can augment the last area commonly used for connection and camaraderie.

Suggested Cures

- Close the curtains at mealtimes.

- Place plants in front of the windows.

- Use a small fish bowl for a centerpiece to keep attention focused toward the table.

- Place floating candles or flowers or revolving holiday decorations in a bowl in the table's center.

- Light candles even in daytime.

- Position a gently rotating fan above the table.

72. Why does a windowless room generate negative feelings or substandard performance?

Because humans are designed biologically to have all their senses engaged

Nature is not inclined to be superfluous. Humans are designed to be efficient, and everything we have is intended to be used. Although we depend on our eyes for much of what we experience, sight is not the only sensor that endows us with messages. We smell, taste, hear, and feel. When one sensorial system is denied stimulation, we feel disenfranchised, even sometimes slightly depressed.

A water fountain and a ticking clock generate a more nurturing and tolerable atmosphere should you have to spend time in a windowless room.

Suggested Cures

Should you be required to spend time in an environment without direct visual, thermal, and audio contact with the outdoors, there are things you can do:

- Have at least three distinctly different colors in the space.

- Make sure two kinds of movement are present, such as a clock's swinging pendulum and a billowing curtain, moving water in a fountain, or a ceiling fan.

- Install ongoing sounds like the hum of machinery, hushed music, or a water feature's trickle or intermittent sounds like a gusting breeze or clocks that chime on the hour.

- Saturate three cotton balls with three unlike scents such as pine in the morning, lemon after lunch, and lavender near day's end. If the windowless room is a work space, just place them in the open on your desk. If you have control over the entire environment, you can circulate them in a scent diffuser.

- Use different cushions on a chair or have several armrests and switch them on a regular basis.

9

How Gathering and Dining Spaces Affect Human Interactions

A great deal of family interaction takes place in the gathering and dining spaces. Thus, these areas have the power to enhance or detract from human interaction. While good feng shui is based on what aesthetically pleases you, its primary focus is on helping you create a vortex for relaxation, communication, self-esteem, and comfort with your highest and best self. We often don't give appropriate consideration to how colors, furniture positioning, and choice of accessories influences us. This chapter is meant to help you keep in mind what to strive for in these important spaces—the ones central to our connection with others that also have the potential to deeply nurture our own needs.

73. How can paths into the main gathering space promote family unity?

When several paths lead to this space

Like the expression "All roads lead to Rome," most paths through a home physically or visually should connect with a commonly used gathering area. A feeling of community is the strength of family life, and it is wise to promote access to the space used most by all members. Even for those living solo, creating easy access to the gathering space supports self-esteem by encouraging them to spend time in what is typically a highly esteemed place in their home.

Passageways can be footpaths or sight lines. Seeing the gathering space from other locations is sufficient as long as there are no visual obstructions.

Pierce a wall to permit a view to the main gathering space, especially when there are not several paths leading there.

Suggested Cures

• Cut a picture frame–sized opening in a wall to permit a view of a gathering space:

> Portholes or round openings encourage conversation and mental activity.
> Horizontal rectangles framing a view stimulate the desire to be part of the ongoing activities.
> Square openings communicate stability.

• Have a similar variety of houseplants located in several spots throughout the home with the largest and most glorious specimen in the gathering space.

• Have everyone's favored items accessible, such as the teenage boy's favorite basketball book, the young child's toys, an adult's reading materials, games, or snacks.

74. What seating configuration is most likely to encourage verbal interaction?

Sitting at right angles to one another

You may have noticed how at social gatherings men will face each other squarely and women are more likely to stand at a slight angle to converse. This is because men are often more comfortable with being aggressive than woman are. Women more often assume the martial arts wisdom of crouching or holding one's body sideways when approaching an enemy. We feel protected when the center of our bodies or our vital organs are sheltered.

Thus seating at right angles feels nonthreatening and encourages nonconfrontational communication. The famous cultural anthropologist, Edward T. Hall, showed us in his book *The Hidden Dimension* that more interaction occurs when chairs are at right angles than when across from each other or side by side. Measuring the rate of communication between people seated in different configurations, he found that the most frequent interactions took place between those who were seated at right angles.

Suggested Cures

If you can't arrange for seating at right angles, try these suggestions.

In gathering spaces

• Install a window seat and place an ottoman at a right angle to it.

• Have an ottoman on wheels convenient to place at right angles to another seat.

• Switch to smaller chairs to accommodate right-angle seating.

• Position what is typically a solo arm or club chair with another to prevent that person from being isolated or commanding more power than is advisable.

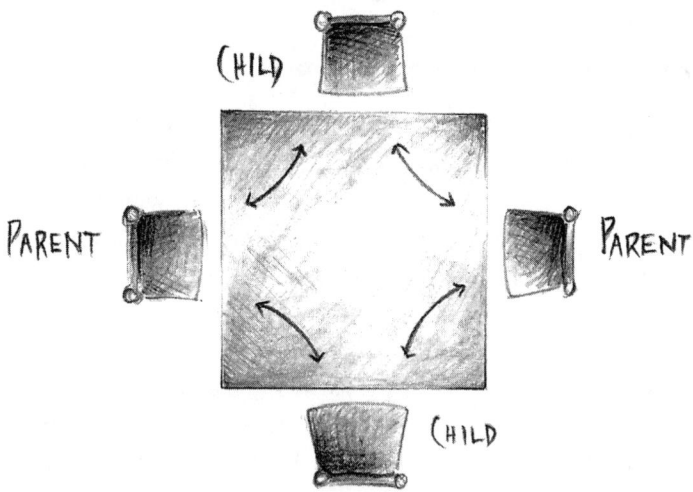

Those seated at right angles to each other are likely to converse most frequently.

- Even when two couches are at right angles to each other, place a small chair at one of the far ends to form another right-angled seating group.

In dining areas

- Seating two children at right angles to their parents provides the best configuration for nonconfrontational communication.

- The middle seat in a row of three chairs should be reserved for someone who is self-confident enough to handle being spoken to least.

75. Why is television detrimental to communication?

Because it invites passivity

A television discourages communication because it allows family members to get used to being entertained without having to exert effort. All that TV requires is passively sitting and watching. Even reading, although isolating when you don't read aloud, requires you to be an active participant because you are required to use mental acuity. Because of its ease and because it focuses attention away from the present circumstances, a TV discourages interaction. A prominent TV located on a wall directly in line with the room's entrance communicates that the main purpose of the room is not interaction. Encouraging exchanges among family and friends rather than supporting passive entertainment ultimately supports conditions that foster contentment.

Suggested Cures

If your TV is across from the room's opening, try these recommendations to lessen its potentially negative impact:

- Move the unit to another wall.

- Place a plant in a stand with wheels in front when the TV is not in use.

Hiding a TV alters a room's use from that of passive entertainment
to that of socializing.

- Suspend a lightweight, easily removable painting to hide the TV.

- Position a lightweight screen in front of the TV.

- Drape a scarf or fabric over the TV.

- Place the TV in an armoire and close the doors when the TV is not
being watched.

76. What furniture arrangement encourages a room's use?

Seats facing the entrance

Like a friend waving you to come over, seating facing the entrance is
inviting. The more you feel seduced by an unspoken implication, the

more likely you are to enter. When there are obstructions, the least bit of resistance to using a space usually wins.

Suggested Cures

To encourage a room's use, be sure the path to the main seating is not obstructed and that the majority of seating faces the entrance. If this is architecturally impossible because there is more than one entrance or because window placement or size of furniture precludes arranging the seating area to face the entrance, here are some remedies to entice people into a gathering space:

- Use vibrant or deep colors on the wall in direct view of the entrance.

- Hang a picture with a distant view across from the entrance.

- Place a significant or slightly-larger-than-normal object on the cocktail table in front of the largest seating unit.

- Direct a higher-wattage light in the center of the floor between seating units, either from an overhead fixture or from a clip-on spot from the wall.

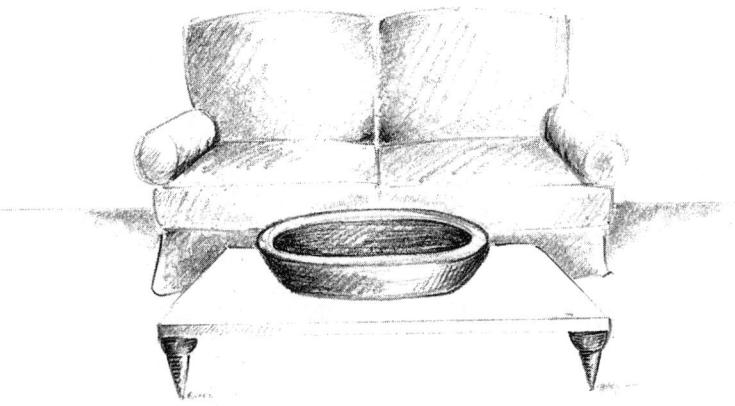

A heavy object on a coffee table is a magnet like the sun is to the planets
and promotes family cohesiveness.

77. What dining room feature contributes to feelings of abundance?

When there are no more chairs around the table than the number of diners

The number of chairs we choose for a dining table often indicates our ideal number of diners. When a family's numbers shrink because the children have moved away or a divorce or death has occurred, allowing the unoccupied chair to remain evokes a sense of discontent, loss, and disquiet.

Suggested Cures

If the table is too large to remove some chairs and you lack the means or desire to purchase a new table, here are ways to reduce the size of the table:

- Place a runner diagonally across the table to reduce a table for six and reposition chairs at one end.

- Use one end of the table as a sculpture stand or occasional table and place art objects on it.

- Adjust overhead lighting to focus on the end of the table used.

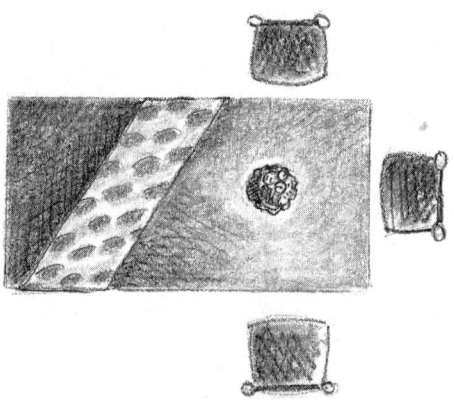

When a table is too large for the typical number of people using it, it communicates a feeling that something is missing; to counteract that, shrink the table by laying a runner on the diagonal.

78. What shape table encourages equality?

Round

Conversation, ideas, and interaction flow with greater ease when people are seated around a circular table, where there is no clear demarcation of personal space. The fluid, curved line does not naturally indicate a stopping point. This makes the people sitting at the table equals, and dialogue is more likely to occur than when two people are right next to each other but some boundary exists—such as between adjacent airplane seats. A round table doesn't impose a structural reason for not being close to another person. And a round table doesn't have a clear "head of the table," so no one person is imbued with more power than the others. All of these factors add to the feeling of equality.

Suggested Cures

Should you not own a round table and feel the benefits could contribute to your family's contentment, here are some ways to approximate the spirit of a circle:

- Arrange a centerpiece in a round bowl and place it on a round cloth in the table's center.

- Position ceiling lights in a circle to cast an obvious circle of light.

- Use a blue tablecloth because of its association with water and the fluidity that is inherent in a circle.

- Cover the table with two cloths of different colors. Use the lighter color on top and fold its edges to approximate a circle.

79. What shape table promotes cohesion for blended families?

Square

With more and more marriages ending in divorce, it is not unlikely that future families will have two or even three sets of children with different biological parents living under one roof. Such a mix is wrought with potential problems such as mixed loyalties and unequal control. Therefore an atmosphere that enhances a sense of togetherness, belonging, and stability makes sense. Being seated around a square table will promote those feelings more than will other shapes.

A square is a shape with all sides equal, so no one has more or less space. Yet the personal space is defined, for the corner of the table delineates each person's space. Should the square be fifty-four inches or larger, two people can sit on every side, and the sense of solidarity remains unchanged, because the overall shape sends the message of stability and unity more than the individual's place.

Suggested Cures

If a square table is not available, here's what to do to help create its spirit:

• If you have a round table, cover it with a square piece of wood to change the shape.

• Purchase or sew square place mats for each family member.

• Place a square area rug under the table.

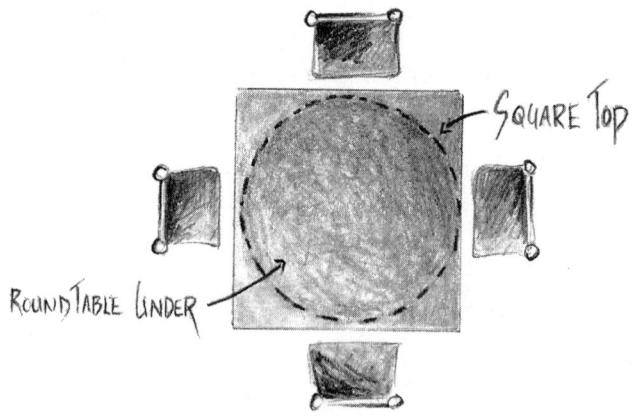

Even if your table is round, you can change it to a square to promote family unity by placing a square surface over the top.

- Provide armless chairs for the people at the head of a rectangular table and chairs with arms for the others.

- Place a square candle on a square cloth at the table's center.

80. What lighting promotes lingering and socializing at a dining table?

Lighting or shadow that encircles the table's top plus the diners while excluding the room's perimeter

If you have ever huddled around a campfire after sundown, you have experienced the camaraderie stimulated by a campfire's light. I remember feeling excited, yet safe during hurricanes because my dad would make a fire in our fireplace and we would gather around its warmth and glow. Instead of being terrified by the threat of impending danger, I would be nourished by my family's presence. Conversely, darkening the area around a table while lighting the perimeter can envelop the diners

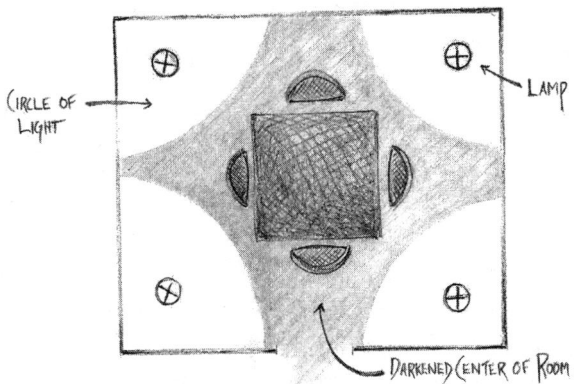

Make the center of the dining room darker and surround the diners in a comfortable blanket of darkness.

in a feeling of being sequestered in a cozy, contained atmosphere. The veil of darkness can, in some cases, be the positive counterpoint to the more typical experience of rooms that are lit uniformly.

Suggested Cures

• To darken the table area, mount channels up from the wall's electrical sockets and affix ceiling lights pointing to perimeter areas.

• To lighten the table area, string rope lights up from a wall outlet and mount them on the ceiling over the table.

• Lower or increase the wattage in bulbs over the dining table until it is either brighter or darker than the surrounding area.

• Should you have an appropriate central fixture, add some pink bulbs—pink light glows with warmth.

• Use an area carpet under the table and chairs several degrees lighter than the existing flooring.

81. What are the benefits of facing a window?

Reducing loneliness and depression and providing inspiration

While windows do focus attention away from what is going on inside, there are specific times when facing a window can be positive. The following life situations lend themselves to facing outside:

Recent loss of a loved one
Being ill and unable to leave the home
Ongoing inclement weather that prevents you from going
  outdoors
Desire to make a life change without the ability to muster actions
  that will set change in motion

A window seat permits an intimate outside view that both inspires and diminishes the feeling of isolation.

Suggested Cures

When lonely

- Build a window seat overlooking your favorite view.
- Purchase casters to make your favorite seat move easily.
- Build a large lazy Susan and place your favorite chair on top.
- Raise your bed's height so you can see easily out a bedroom window.

82. What table shape encourages unhurried dining?

Square

A square dining table encourages diners to linger. With all sides of equal size, a square is the most stable shape, and when seated at a square table everybody is equally well positioned to participate in the conversation.

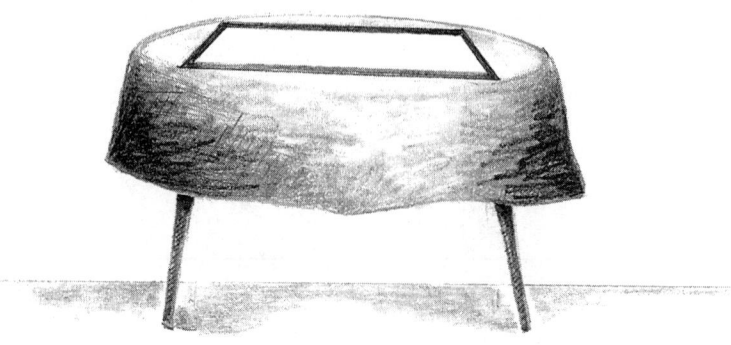

Place or sew a square shape on a table covering should you have a round table, to foster both conversation and lingering at mealtimes to socialize.

If you have ever sat at a long rectangular table with lively talk at the opposite end, you know what I mean. You are out of the loop. However, at a square table each person has the same potential to be included and the atmosphere of intimacy makes us wish to linger.

Suggested Cures

• Reshape a round table by sewing a square shape on the tablecloth or purchase a square of glass, wood, or plastic and lay it over the round surface.

• Reshape a rectangular table by:

Placing a long scarf runner diagonally across the table, making it appear as two triangles

Placing a row of place mats or a bolt of cloth across one end in a color that contrasts with everything else on the table

10

Ways to Enhance Sex and Sleep

I t is obvious to most of us that sleep and sexuality are central to thriving, but what is not apparent is the role the environment has in these needs. If you have ever slipped into an undisturbed slumber while floating in a hammock on a picture-perfect day or shared kisses with a loved one while lounging on a soft surface in the warmth of a fireplace, you have experienced how place acts as an enhancer to sleep and sexuality. The cures in this chapter alter environmental ingredients to benefit sleep and sexuality.

83. Where should a bed be positioned to create the best ambience for sleep?

At least three feet away from any TV, whether in the same room or in an adjacent room on the other side of the wall that the bed is against

In the most literal sense a bed is a nest, a place to let down your guard and be totally at ease. The body recovers from the stresses of living when it sleeps. Getting a good night's rest is not only enjoyable but also healthy. We need a deeply relaxing environment to support this.

As already said, the best environment for deep sleep is when the bed faces the entrance of the room but is not directly in front of it. So long as you can move your head at about a thirty-degree angle and still see the door, the bed is positioned in the best direction. But that's not all.

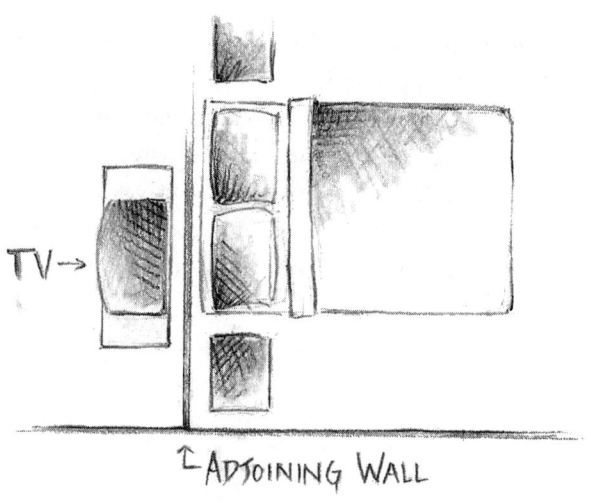

To create the best ambience for sleeping, don't position a bed against a wall
that has a TV, even when the TV is in the next room.

A bed should not have a television positioned on either side of the wall against which the bed leans. Since our bodies are electrical systems and a TV emits electricity continually, even when turned off, we are constantly bombarded by electric and magnetic fields if we sleep in a bed in such a position. Walls do not stop electrical or magnetic currents, and if a bed is within three feet of a TV set you will be subjected to electrical charges all night. Just moving a bed away from a wall with a television against it has in my feng shui practice relieved many clients' sleep problems.

Suggested Cures

If you can't distance your bed from the television, these other suggestions can be equally effective:

- Unplug the television before going to bed.

- Install an on/off switch, the same kind used for lights, that turns off the fuse box segment in which the TV's electric outlet is connected.

84. Where should a bed be positioned to encourage sexuality?
In a place that ensures visual and auditory privacy

In general, sensuality can be augmented by being relaxed enough to let your guard down and feel emotionally and physically at ease. Being where you might be seen or heard is hardly conducive to letting go. But during the stages of life when you are living with children or others, a closed door may not be enough to make you feel completely at ease.

Suggested Cures

For visual privacy
- Add an interior curtain under the doorjamb on the opposite side of the door's swing.

- If your bed is at right angles to the entrance door, position a dresser at right angles to the door and suspend a large picture over it.

- Purchase or fashion a canopy bed and hang or loop fabric over the railings that is easy to open and close.

For auditory privacy

- Pad a shared wall with porous material like cork, foam, or other soundproofing materials.

- Reposition the bed away from a wall adjacent to another occupied bedroom.

- Put a water feature or white noise machine in the adjacent bedroom.

- Hang a rug or tapestry against an unbuffered wall.

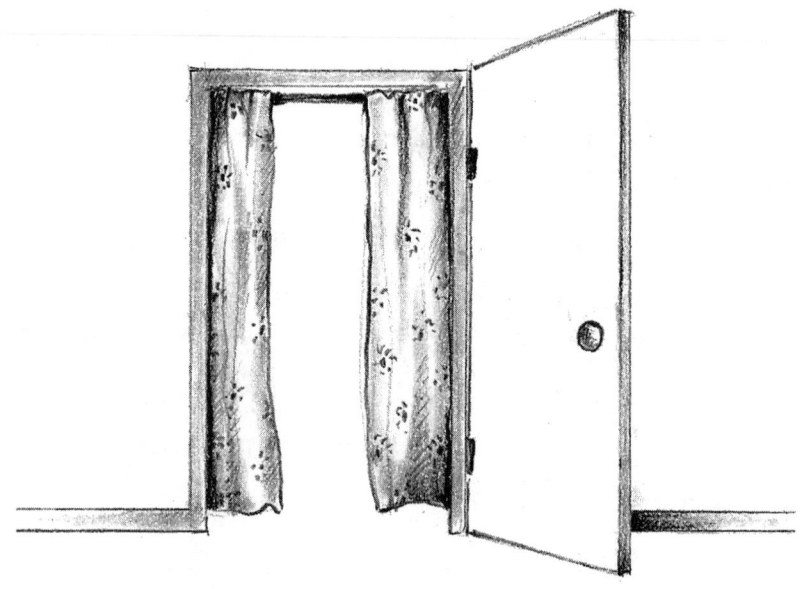

Adding a curtain over the bedroom's entrance door can provide an additional buffer and create an atmosphere more conducive to sexuality.

85. What scents induce sensuality?

Sandalwood, patchouli, and rose

What words would you use to describe sulfur? Pungent, dank, and offensive? Do those words truly convey the specific olfactory experience? Smell, our oldest sense, is connected with primal instincts and emotions, not intellectual processes, making it the hardest of all sensory experiences to describe.

The scents of sandalwood, patchouli, and rose lead our emotions to sensuality—yet there are nuances. Read the differences and use the scents that fit. Remember, if a scent evokes an unpleasant memory, no matter what its universal positive characteristics are, don't use it. If you disliked a teacher who wore sandalwood, it is highly probable that in adulthood you will be turned off by a lover who wears that fragrance.

Suggested Cures

• Diffuse sandalwood to feel less self-conscious about your body,

• Spray your pillow with patchouli to reconnect with an energized sensuality.

• Dispense rose as an elixir or aphrodisiac.

• Burn sandalwood incense to diminish the tyranny of the intellect.

• Light rose-scented candles to restore trust.

Add patchouli oil to either water or a carrier oil and create a pillow spray
that will energize sensuality.

86.   What mirror placement negatively affects sexual relationships?

Seeing yourself in the mirror when seated in bed

Most of us already struggle with self-consciousness and insecurity over our appearance. We don't need a mirror pushed in our face at times when we want to feel confident and relaxed—especially since it's a rare individual who can resist checking out his or her image when a mirror is right there. Looking at your own reflection also diverts your attention away from your partner. To create the best atmosphere for sexuality, remove mirrors from central locations in your bedroom.

Suggested Cures

Should a mirror be necessary for dressing and grooming, you can reposition or camouflage the mirror in various ways:

- Hang a mirror on the wall behind the entrance door.

- Suspend a mirror inside a closet door.

If a freestanding mirror faces the bed, tilt it upward to prevent you from being distracted and potentially unempowered.

- Situate a lightweight screen in front of an existing mirror.

- Replace with a three-way mirror that folds shut.

- If the mirror is on a tilting stand, tip it up when not in use.

- Replace a mirror over a dresser with a romantic picture.

87. Which feature above a bed can cause tension and thus dilute sexual enjoyment?

A ceiling beam

Beams are the bones of a building and critical to a structure's integrity. In the same way that picnicking under a looming bolder would not be comforting, lying under a beam can communicate danger. If you live in an area where earthquakes or tornadoes are prevalent, you likely will feel even more threatened. We tense up when at risk, and if you have ever

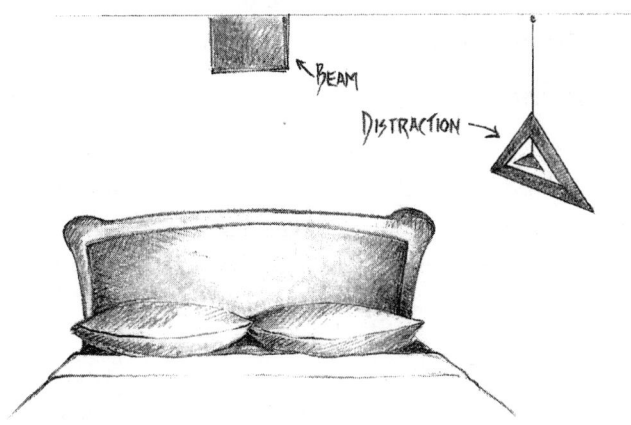

A moving object or a triangular shape captures the eye's attention, mitigating some of the negative effect of a beam over a bed.

clenched your teeth, bitten your fingernails, or broken out in perspiration when something made you nervous, you know how antithetical to relaxed sensuality this involuntary reaction is. Beams above a bed create just enough subconscious strain to cause muscle tension and interfere with feeling completely relaxed during sexual contact.

Suggested Cures

If beams are visible, here are some ways to mitigate their negative influence:

- Purchase a four-poster bed and stretch fabric over the top four poles.

- Paint the beams the same color as the ceiling.

- Mirror the underside of the beam if it is narrow enough that you won't see your image in full.

- If beams are not attached to the ceiling, mount a mobile or a triangular object above the beam. Or, if the beam and ceiling are contiguous, hang the mobile or object in your sight line from the bed.

88. How can you lessen the negative effect of a bed's placement in front of a window?

Install a headboard that is completely solid and opaque

Any concern or distraction compromises your ability to let go as you need to do for both sleep and sexual activity. If your bed is in front of a window, you won't be able to help feeling vulnerable. The fact that you are separated from the outside world by only a thin glass membrane may make you feel exposed and even endangered.

Suggested Cures

Although it is best not to place a bed in front of a window, sometimes it is unavoidable, in which case you can buy a headboard that has no

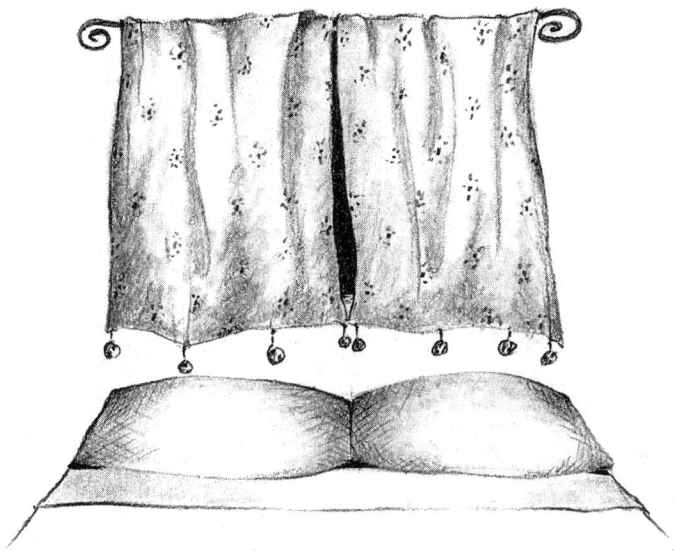

If you sleep with a bed against a window and cannot reposition it, attach lightweight bells to the hem to reassure you that the noise will signal any penetration from outside.

open design or slats. If you prefer not to go that route, however, there are alternatives:

- Install wooden shutters with latches.

- Cover a pierced headboard with a caftan or heavy throw to give it a solid appearance.

- Hang a bell on the part of the window that is likely to be opened.

- Attach a bell to the hem of the existing curtains.

- Hang two sets of curtains, one transparent and light, the other an opaque, thicker fabric, and close the opaque set when you need to feel out of harm's way.

89. What view hinders romance in a bedroom?

A toilet

The romance of a bathtub filled with perfectly formed scented bubbles and a glass of champagne perched on the ledge is the stuff of sexy advertisements, but the fact is that the first thing seen in most bathrooms is not a luxurious tub. In our culture, we learn to feel comfortable using the toilet only in private. So being able to see the toilet from your bed is about as sexy as scrubbing dirty dishes.

Suggested Cures

Should the architecture of your home make rearranging impossible, here are some suggestions:

For a bathroom that has an open passage rather than a door

- Hang a lightweight curtain in the corridor's opening.

- Hinge a folding screen across the opening.

- Place a large leafy plant in front of the opening even if it requires walking around the plant to enter.

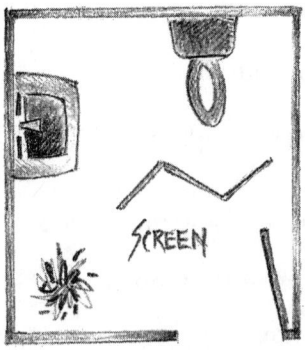

Place a three-paneled screen in front of the door to hide a view of the toilet when the door is opened.

For a bathroom that allows a view of the toilet from the bed when the door is open

• Mount a self-closing hinge on the bathroom door to ensure the door shuts automatically.

• If the door opens into the bedroom, hang two panels of fabric across the inside of the door.

• Install a folding screen in front of the toilet if it is in direct line with the door.

90. What bed position will make you feel exposed and thus uptight?

The bed directly across from the entrance door

A bed directly across from the entrance to the room can make you feel uncomfortably exposed and vulnerable to potential embarrassment. Having even a remote fear of exposure is not conducive to sleeping or feeling sexually free.

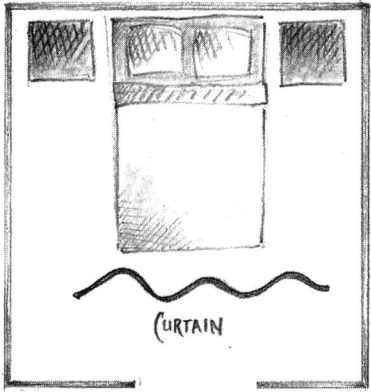

If your bed is directly across from the room's entrance, mount a curtain at the foot of a bed to preserve a completely private atmosphere.

Your bedroom should have a buffer zone between the threshold and your bed. Ideally the layout would require you to turn slightly left or right and walk at least three steps from the door to the bed.

Suggested Cures

If the room's size doesn't permit such a path, and it's not possible to move the bed to the ideal position, there are other ways to evoke the same feeling:

• Loop a bell over the entrance doorknob to signal when someone is about to enter.

• Position a screen at the foot of the bed to block a direct view.

• Suspend a pole at the foot of the bed and hang a curtain the same width as the bed.

91. What color can spoil sensuality and should be avoided around a bed?

Yellow

While yellow is the color of cheer and optimism, it unfortunately gives the human body a sickly look. Teeth and the whites of the eyes appear less than healthy when yellow is reflected. You don't have to avoid yellow altogether in the bedroom, but do take care where you place it. Avoid using yellow near the head of a bed, including the wall behind the bed, sheets, pillowcases, and lampshades.

Suggested Cures

If yellow is currently near the head of the bed and you want a quick fix before repainting the room, here's what you can do:

• Acquire a red/pink lightbulb and shine it on the yellow surfaces.

• Install a curtain across the yellow wall and close it at bedtime.

• If you have a four-poster bed, drape a pink, rose, or burgundy throw across the top.

• Cover an extra-large pillow with a red pillowcase and prop it up against the yellow wall.

92. What colors create the most sensuous atmosphere in a bedroom?

Rose, salmon or pink, and light orange

Women know that a touch of blusher on the cheeks enhances their appearance. The tones that have a bit of red complement the skin and make us look healthier. When surrounded by those tones in a softly lit setting, we are physically enhanced. And feeling beautiful lends itself to sexuality. Consider how you feel and act when empowered by what you are wearing. When romance is in the air, being surrounded with colors that flatter rather than detract seems sensible.

A lightweight rose-toned fabric suspended from dowels alters an incandescent light's color to one that flatters. (Be sure to spray the draped material used with a fire retardant.)

Suggested Cures

Should repainting or redecorating not be an immediate option, here are some alternatives:

• Dye existing pale pillowcases red tones (Rit dyes are inexpensive and easy to use).

• Purchase tinted bulbs for lamps next to the head of the bed or in an overhead fixture.

• Purchase fabric or an area rug and hang on a dowel over a light.

• Install a curtain in rose, salmon or pink, or light orange across a wall and close when the siren of romance calls.

93. What accessory stimulates romance?

Scented candles

Do you remember whether your first romantic experience happened on a mild spring day when the lilacs were just blooming or on a cold winter's night with the scent of pine wafting from the Christmas tree? The scents associated with an experience of heightened feeling are forever linked with that emotion. Therefore, replicating the scent remembered from a positive romantic experience can promote the same kinds of feelings that were aroused when those first sparks flew.

On the other hand, scents associated with a negative memory or association should be avoided even when that scent is recommended in product literature. The popular scent lavender, for example, is good for almost whatever ails you, but if your obnoxious cousin wore lavender cologne you would not feel sexy with its aroma surrounding you. In fact just the opposite would be true. It is with these words of caution that I suggest the following aphrodisiacs, which can steer the soul toward romance.

You can accommodate each partner's needs by making individualized sachets filled with scents and slipping it into each person's pillows.

Suggested Cures

• Jasmine candles are an excellent aphrodisiac for those who find it difficult to express themselves owing to lack of self-confidence.

• Patchouli linen spray can lull the mind and warm the body for those with a high degree of mental pressure.

• Ylang-ylang incense or body oil can release sexual anxiety.

• A ginger sachet in a pillow sack can turn you on and energize you.

Ways a Home Can Support Parenting

Of course, good parenting takes a lot more than a felicitous environment, but because parenting can be difficult and certainly can always be improved upon, it is a good idea to call into place as many tools as possible. Feng shui offers insights to improve what is perhaps our most important life function—to lend support to our progeny to grow into contented, fulfilled adults. By examining the space children have the majority of their experiences in, we can ferret out those conditions that can detract from their development and add conditions that will help them flourish.

94. What architectural feature may frighten a child at night?

A window

Although by day windows are the TVs of nature, at night they can make a child feel vulnerable to threats both real and imagined that may be lurking in the dark outside. When the child's bed is in front of a window, your son or daughter may balk at bedtime, exclaiming "I don't want to go to bed" or "I can't fall asleep" or "There's a monster outside." How your child reacts to the windows in his or her bedroom may depend on what they frame at night, however. A starry sky surrounding a silhouette of skyscrapers from a high-rise window may appeal to your child, while tree branches blowing in the wind may look like intruding arms or scary faces.

When a light illuminates what is outside, a child will be less likely to think the oak tree is a ghost.

Suggested Cures

If there is any chance that your child will find the view outside the bedroom window frightening, try these cures:

• Make sure the curtains are closed or that a child faces away from the windows when in bed.

• If the child needs reassurance that nothing is threatening or lurking outside, position a light to shine outside over each window at night.

• Use easy-to-manipulate window treatments.

95. What can you do to your home to promote a child's attentiveness or focus?

Eliminate as many distractions as possible

When I was in grade school, I would make an effort to sit near my classroom's wall of windows. Bored with school, I chose that vantage point so I would have an alternative to listening to the teacher. The action outside triggered my fantasies. It may have been the face of a driver traveling down the street or the feat of a squirrel leaping from branch to branch. My view from the window was the distraction that made it possible for me to avoid participating in school.

While a child needs a stimulating and eclectic environment, clutter on surfaces can serve as distractions.

It is equally important for parents to make sure their child's typical view of them not be compromised by distractions in the distance, especially in areas of communication like gathering or dining rooms.

Suggested Cures

- Move any mirrors that are within view from the child's vantage point.

- Do not let a child's chair face a window.

- Be sure that you are seated with your back to a wall.

- Don't hang pictures with a great deal of detail or an engaging, active scene within a child's view.
  - Eliminate clutter on tabletops.

96. Why are children often bored at home?

Because most homes don't have enough areas devoted to different activities

Boredom can be defined as the reaction to a lack of options. Humans thrive best when surrounded by variety. Children have not yet developed firm preferences, so they need to be able to explore. This helps them uncover essential attributes of self as well as gain confidence and comfort in diverse situations. Providing distinct areas in which they can pursue a variety of activities will stimulate a child's natural curiosity and enhance the child's contentment.

Suggested Cures

- *Quiet zone:* Devote a cozy corner or niche in a room where it is comfortable to read, daydream, and listen to music or simply nap. Use floor pillows or an extra area rug for comfort or a draped table under which a child can be out of view. A toy/book shelf and a device for listening to music might be placed nearby. Do not have reds or greens within view from this area.

Using a plastic toddler's pool indoors as a defined messy area allows children to explore paints, water, and other gooey, gummy stuff while containing mess.

- *Discovery zone:* This should be an area with enough empty space to easily access items for a child to explore. A canvas area rug over existing flooring may give a child the confidence to sort rocks, take apart an old alarm clock, or cut out paper forms without harming the surroundings.

- *Making a mess zone:* Playing with water or gooey stuff is fun for children. Use a small plastic swimming pool to allow a child to sit indoors and play with liquids, paints, and other messy but fun materials.

- *Imagination zone:* This should be an area with lots of "stuff" and no passive equipment (TV) where building, inventing stories, and re-creating daydreams is possible. Use a treasure chest to hold these things. A tent or curtain for privacy can be the catalyst for this zone.

97. What bedroom features might increase a child's fear of monsters?

Closets and concealed spaces

Children rarely discover goblins and other terrifying inventions of the imagination sitting on the living room sofa, especially when the room is filled with family members. Monsters typically come from unknown sources or tend to hide, revealing their presence in rather erratic ways. Therefore concealed, out-of-sight places like closets, the area outside the blackened night's window, and poorly lit hallways are often suspect.

Suggested Cures

• Keep closet doors open, especially at night. Let your child decide if the closet light needs to remain on in the evening, or if just the availability of the light is sufficient to dissipate any concern.

• Make sure closets are organized and that items are not stacked behind one another.

A slide bolt on a closet door can give a child assurance that a monster will not emerge from its depths.

• Mount an exterior light outside a child's window to eliminate the black-hole look.

• Place a flashlight on a bedside nightstand.

• Keep hallway lights on.

• Use light-colored paint on walls (yellow is particularly good for brightening even a darkened room).

• Purchase packs of glow-in-the-dark stars and mount them around the bed.

• Affix a slide bolt that the child can operate on the outside of the closet.

98. How can you entice children to engage in activities other than watching television or playing computer games?

Set up a room where all senses are engaged and provide special options

Today's children often spend far too much time watching TV or playing computer games. In some ways these activities offer a wider range of stimulation than the typical home offers. What is so seductive is their compelling sensorial involvement.

TV has larger-than-life characters engaged in far more actions than are typical in real life. Colors, movement, and other visual phenomena are many and varied. Sounds are exaggerated and diverse. Events and actions take place at a clip far exceeding real-life speeds. In the same way that we adults are often drawn to rubberneck at an accident scene, children are drawn to the sensational offerings of TV.

You can compete with this irresistible attraction by creating an environment packed with interactive choices that encourage children to immerse themselves in their own world of make-believe rather than that of the TV producers.

Suggested Cures

• Put your TV in a less-frequented room. When children are young, they tend to want to share space with their parents, so locating the TV where you spend little time will minimize their exposure to this passive form of entertainment.

• Create small cloistered niches not unlike tents and fill them with books, a microscope for examining small objects, or other interactive objects that aid children in focusing on small items.

Children love high-up spaces, so having a loft play area will entice a child to spend time on alternatives to TV watching.

• Suspend a hammock or platform and fill it with playing or reading activities.

• Make an indoor water area by positioning a small wading pool on a large tarp in a room or under the dining room table.

• Allow a child to participate in cooking, preparing ingredients, or inventing recipes.

• Build a balcony around a room connected with ladder bridges for large motor activities that will not mess anything up.

• Place a Hula Hoop outside on the ground and have the children fill it with whatever you can think of—as many bugs as they can find, as many different rocks, different-colored grains in sand, and so forth. Be inventive.

99. How can a home's decor reduce a child's inappropriately charged activity?

Tone down deeply saturated colors, patterns with stripes, strong light or scents, and loud or fast music

In feng shui we call anything that stimulates activity *yang*. Childhood is primarily a yang stage. Children are generally much more active than adults and it is appropriate for them to engage in a high level of physical activity. However, the amount of yang stimulation in a home can be reduced if this behavior reaches inappropriate levels.

Too often we decorate children's rooms in ways that mimic their highly charged behavior, using bright colors, strong lights, and intense pictures. For a child who is naturally active and highly charged, this decor will only increase the intensity and activity level. For that reason, it is important to add yin colors, shapes, scents, sounds, and textures. Just as quietly singing a lullaby can create an atmosphere in which a child can decompress and relax, decorating a space with yin can counter a child's normally yang activity level.

Suggested Cures

Chapter 1 offers more details on yin characteristics versus yang characteristics, but here are some specific suggestions for children's spaces:

- Use light colors, especially salmons, blues, purples, and tans.

- Use prints with squares or square repeats.

Light colors, squares, low furnishings, firm seating, and a cool atmosphere create a quiet atmosphere, which balances the high activity level of most children.

- Opt for furniture that is low to the ground, without tall spindly legs.

- Use a square area rug even if there is wall-to-wall carpeting.

- Have scents of herbs rather than flowers dispersed in the child's space.

- Choose firm rather than bouncy seating.

- Keep the space slightly cool.

100. What can cause or exacerbate health problems in children?

Any product that emits volatile organic compounds (VOCs) or electro or magnetic charges, houses bacteria, or contains fibers with bleach

With respiratory illnesses, cancers, and other illnesses on the rise, it is time to consider the environmental responsibility for this increase. While air pollution, food additives, and electro and magnetic fields are culprits that we cannot single-handedly change, there are some precautions that parents can take to reduce environmental stresses.

Here are some things parents can do to reduce environmental health threats to children:

Suggested Cures

- Do not position a bed against a wall with any electrical appliance on either side of the wall.

- Avoid using a baby monitor or, if it is essential, hang it a few feet away from the crib.

- Rather than having wall-to-wall carpeting in a child's bedroom, which can be a breeding ground for dust and mold, use an all-cotton throw rug that is machine washable.

- Keep a window slightly ajar year-round for air exchange.

- Use cleaning and washing products without bleach or formaldehydes.

- Use VOC-free paints (see the last entry in Resources for more information).

101. Why should teenagers be allowed to paint their room black or purple?

Because it parallels their exploration of self

Adolescence is a time of exploration, discovery, and accumulation of self-knowledge. Clearly no longer a child but also not yet an adult, the teenager seeks answers to a raft of pressing questions, the principal one being "What will I become?" These unknowns are expressed by the colors black and purple. Black, the absorption of all colors, does not send

Make teenagers happy by allowing them to use purple or black in their bedrooms, and make yourself happy by not having to worry about painting over these deep colors later on by mounting fabric over the walls rather than painting them.

a clear-cut message. In feng shui we say that black is the color of mystery. Purple, on the other hand, is not visible in the color spectrum—as in ultraviolet light—and represents that which is not commonplace and cannot be experienced easily. Thus the choice of black and purple relays the questions lying in the depth of a teenager's soul.

Suggested Cures

If you simply can't stand the idea of black or purple walls in your home, try these alternatives that will allow your maturing child freedom of self-expression:

- Purchase cloth in those colors and tack it to the walls.

- Find a large poster with mostly black and purple or buy a few copies of the same one and repeat it a few times to use as wallpaper.

- Hang curtains in these colors around the room over the walls.

AFTERWORD

WHAT IS SO interesting about feng shui is that once you understand how messages are communicated in an environment you can start manipulating them in the same way you might accessorize an outfit. In the same way that a gold, silver, or feather pin sets a tone on a basic solid-colored suit, you can tweak a room or an area to send the message you want to deliver. But feng shui is only half of the recipe. Self-knowledge is the other half. It is only when you fully explore your needs and desires that you can make choices that will help you achieve the greatest good for you. First you must assess what you need. Then you can use your environment as a tool to reach your goals.

I remember how one of my tenth-grade classrooms changed depending on whether it was the English teacher or the history teacher who was holding sway at the time. The lighting, colors, windows, doors, and furniture placement remained the same from period to period, but my English teacher was able to instill a tone of seriousness into the room, while under the aegis of my history teacher later in the day the space became a veritable funhouse. I hope this book has helped you understand how much influence the character of your spaces has on you, but please don't underestimate the power of your input into a space.

Knowing what you want and need, and understanding how different ways of shaping a room can affect your thoughts, emotions, and actions, can bring a swiftness and ease to reaching your goals that will astound you. When I wanted to write my first feng shui book, I had not written a single published word as an adult. I needed a jump-start, inspirational fuel to drive my optimism and self-confidence to begin the process. I used my home to help me reach toward these goals, altering spaces that didn't support the kind of optimism and devotion to hard work that I knew I needed and creating spaces that would inspire me while dampening the anxiety so often associated with risk.

It worked for me, and it can work for you. With this, my eighth book on feng shui in eight years, I know full well the power we have at our fingertips that can help us shape our life's dreams.

Remember that it's not the dream per se; it's the dreamer who must make it happen. You have every right to expect to be self-confident, worry-free and stress-free, vibrant, healthy, and content, as well as to love and be loved in return. Your habitat has the potential to turn these yearnings into reality. Feng shui offers you a way to create an unencumbered pathway toward becoming your highest and best self. And that is what a good life is.

BIBLIOGRAPHY

Ackerman, Diane. *A Natural History of the Senses.* New York: Random House, 1990.

Birren, Faber. *Color Psychology and Color Therapy*, Secaucus, NJ: Citadel Press, 1961.

Campbell, Don. *The Mozart Effect.* New York: Avon, 1997.

Gallagher, Winifred. *The Power of Place.* New York: Simon and Schuster, 1993.

Hall, Edward T. *The Hidden Dimension*, New York: Doubleday, 1990.

Hirsch, Dr. Alan R. *Scentsational Weight Loss.* New York: Simon and Schuster, 1998.

Liberman, Jacob. *Light: Medicine of the Future.* Sante Fe, NM: Inner Traditions, 1990.

Mojay, Gabriel. *Aromatherapy for the Healing Spirit.* Sante Fe, NM: Inner Traditions, 2000.

Resources

Aroma Beautiful

988 Aldersbrook Road

London, Ontario N6G 4N5

Canada

(519) 471-4496

E-fax: 1-419-844-5209

E-mail: aromabeautiful@aol.com

Website: http://www.aromabeautiful.com

High-grade selections of natural essential oils

Demeter Fragrance Library

83 Second Avenue

New York, NY 10003

(212) 473-3450

Website: www.fashion-planet.com

Amazing array of scents

Feng Shui Institute International
7547 Bruns Court
Canal Winchester, OH 43110
Website: www.fengshuiinstituteinternational.com
(614) 837-8370
Information on qualified feng shui professionals and classes
    nationwide

Feng Shui Institute of America
PO Box 488
Wabasso, FL 32970
(888) 488-FSIA
Website: www.Windwater.com
E-mail: Windwater8@aol.com
Feng shui professional training

Linda Parks
922 Elmwood Avenue
Evanston, IL 60202
Declutter expert

Soul Essentials
PO Box 8
Wabasso, FL 32970
(561) 589-9900
Website: www.fengshuiusa.com
"I Feel Full," a scent designed to suppress appetite

Helmut Ziehe
Institute of Bau-Biologie & Ecology
1401 A Cleveland Street
Clearwater, FL 33755
(727) 461-4371
Website: www.bau-biologieusa.com
Information on creating healthy conditions in a home

INDEX